Guide for the Pissed-Off Job-Seeker

Guide for the Pissed-Off Job-Seeker

✦

Angry? Good!
Use That Anger to Get Work!

By David Abel
As told to
Irv Zuckerman

iUniverse, Inc.
New York Lincoln Shanghai

Guide for the Pissed-Off Job-Seeker
Angry? Good! Use That Anger to Get Work!

iUniverse, Inc.

For information address:
iUniverse, Inc.
2021 Pine Lake Road, Suite 100
Lincoln, NE 68512
www.iuniverse.com

ISBN: 0-595-31477-5

Printed in the United States of America

Contents

Introduction ix

David Abel is someone just like you.

Part 1: Where does it start? 1

Part of my anger at being fired started with the way it was done. The rest, when I had to tell other people what had happened.

Part 2: Anxiety is contagious, and its symptom is anger. 4

I made a list of everything and everyone I was angry at. This didn't cool my anger; instead it focused its energy.

Part 3: Putting my anger to work. 6

I learned to keep asking 3 questions: Who, exactly, am I angry at? What was done or not done to cause it? What would it take to appease it?

Part 4: Getting good letters of reference. 8

To make sure, I wrote my own. Here's one example, and what I learned about myself while writing it.

Part 5: Learning how to blow my horn. 12

Why should I have limited myself to only one letter of reference when I have a number of skills? Here's yet another example

Part 6: It helps to get angry at—yourself. 15

I had to ask myself some pretty hard questions. The toughest was why I hadn't organized a job-search campaign before I started running off in all directions.

Part 7: How I found the people I needed. 17

Simple. I asked the people who were preventing me from getting through to them, what it would take to get through to them. Here's the dialogue that worked for me.

Part 8: Developing Contact Communication. 22

A million resumes go out every morning, only to be dumped. I had to develop a different way of getting attention. Here are some examples.

Part 9: Finding contacts at job fairs.. 27

The average job fair is a meat market. Here's the dialogue I used to turn them it into effective Contact Communication.

Part 10: Finding contacts at trade shows 30

I crashed every trade show I could get to—regardless of the specialty. Here's the question that paid off in personal contacts.

Part 11: Finding contacts through the trade press. 32

I learned that well-known people aren't sure if they've met me or not. What better way to set the stage for a 'reunion?'

Part 12: Making the Follow-up Call. 36

So many different responses meant that a lousy ad libber (like me) needed a script. Here's the one that worked best.

Part 13: Conducting a Contact Conversation: 43

This was nothing like my usual thanks-for-coming-in-and-we'll-call-you job interview. In fact, the J-word never came up.

Part 14: Asking the one question I had promised to ask. 47

I had just one question to ask, but I had to set the stage for it. Here's the script I used.

Part 15: The skill of taking good notes: 49

Who would have thought that taking notes at each Contact Conversation could be so important? These are mine, word for word.

Part 16: The return of the ego.. 62

The way I got fired made me doubt my value. But as I learned the criteria for getting work, I found I could meet them!

Part 17: Listening under pressure. 64

Wait a minute! Did this contact just tell me there was a possibility here? I was so tense; I missed it the first time around. But not the second.

Part 18: The 'resume' my contact helped me to write. 67

Getting away from the standard resume really upset the group—until they had a chance to study the sample.

Part 19: Getting closer to getting work by following up. 76

While I wanted to express my gratitude, what I really wanted was another meeting. This is the letter that helped me get it.

Part 20: Follow the yellow brick road 80

I don't live anywhere near Kansas, but I now have a much better idea about how to travel the road toward my own objectives.

Part 21: Show me the money. 82

Initiating the contact was more work than waiting for the ad, but then, I was not only at the head of the line, there was no line.

Part 22: The DOW (Discussion Of Work) 86

When I found myself closing in on work, I had to discipline myself to stick to the procedure that had gotten me that far in the first place.

Part 23: Closing the deal. 94

There comes a time in the Contact Conversation when asking for work is the thing to do—as long as you can do it without actually asking for work.

Part 24: Putting anger to work. 96

Sometimes I got angry at the contact. Sometimes I got angry at myself. But there's no law against using your anger to try again.

Part 25: The contact is at risk, too. 99

I was so focused on the fact that if I didn't get work I'd be in trouble, that I almost missed helping the contact to hire me. Almost.

Part 26: Negotiating the arrangement. 104

Every contact wanted more of something. Once I found out what that was, I was able to negotiate from strength.

Part 27: Trouble shooting. 109

Not everything goes smoothly. That's why there's a 'trouble-shooting' section in any good documentation. Here's mine.

Introduction

This isn't a suspense novel so I'll tell you how it ends right off. Starting with every handicap a job-seeker could suffer in the way of age, past experience and qualifications, I got a better deal than even I had hoped for.

This isn't a how-to book, either. This is what happened to *me*. I made a number of mistakes. I also made a number of discoveries. The most important discovery was that if I wanted help—and, believe me, I needed help—I had to learn how to ask for it.

If I had any advice to pass on, it would be this: You have nothing to lose! Do whatever you like. Be as outrageous as you like. Some people will hate it. Some people will like it. The people who like it will give you work. That's it.

David Abel

By his own admission, David had trouble talking about himself. He had read my first book on the subject of job-search, (HIRE POWER, Putnam/Perigee,) and felt it needed an update to meet the current situation. When David asked for my help, I asked for his. The result is this word-for-word journal of his experiences from beginning to end. The only change from the truth is his last name. For reasons of privacy and aptness, we chose Abel, the first person in recorded history to become a victim because he failed to realize what was going on. You'll see why.

Irv Zuckerman

P.S. There are those publishers who said this book was too 'quirky' for them to know how to market. I took that as a compliment. From David's experience, the conventional resume/cover letter/interview approach doesn't do too well in this job market. Quirky is what it took. It wasn't an easy transition for David to make, but as you will see, he had no choice.

A personal note:

I've been a researcher, writer and lecturer in the field of job-search for more than twenty years. Yet, it was never how I earned my living. My vocation was running a consulting firm specializing in people management—helping companies to be more effective in how they hired, inspired and fired. My clients were 26 of the world's major corporations, from whom I learned a great deal about employment practices. My books, articles and lectures have reached more than 100,000 job-seekers. Welcome aboard.

Part 1:
Where does it start?

All the weeks of sitting in a damp church basement surrounded by the other members of what turned out to be my encounter/support/networking/depressing group were not completely wasted. Aside from learning that group suffering is not for me, I did pick up one idea that turned out to be priceless: keep a journal of what happens every day **and how I felt about it.** It wasn't easy. Not being one to admit many of my feelings, much less parade them on a page, I literally did not know what to say. That is, I did know, but I didn't want to know, if you know what I mean.

Then, when the weeks passed without a real ray of hope—much less a real offer—I thought what the hell. No one will ever see these thoughts but me. So I set them down: a few from memory and the rest as they happened. Now you're seeing them. Perhaps it will encourage you to do the same. If it worked for someone like me who started out with three strikes against him—over age, over-qualified and out of practice (since it had been years since I last looked for a job), the chances are good that it will work for you.

On May 1st, I got fired.

The shoe didn't drop, the ax didn't fall, or anything like that. My boss told me the people in HR wanted to see me. Since I had never even met the people in HR—I'm not even sure we had an HR department when I came aboard 15 years ago—there was a nanosecond where I wondered what this was all about. Then the way my boss disappeared in a hurry told me all I wanted to know—not that I really wanted to know it.

The woman behind the desk I was directed to was a little younger than my daughter. The look on her face was one I had seen before, when Suzy had blown an exam or a date turned out to be a dud. But in this case, the HR person wasn't the one who needed sympathy and understanding. It was me.

First there was the shuffling of forms. Should I take a seat meanwhile? Should I just stand there? I'd never been canned before so I didn't know the protocol. And, as it turned out, neither did she. While I stood there, she didn't actually talk to me. She just read from a page that, as of today, May 1, I was no longer in the employ of Scrooge and Company. (The name, of course, is made up, but the event isn't.) My position of Deputy Director of Education had been "terminated as a result of a reorganization." I was to turn in my ID and my office key. I would receive one week of severance pay for every year of employment starting immediately, and my health insurance coverage would be kept in force for the same period. In addition, office space on the fourth floor had been assigned for the use of excessed personnel, and the outplacement firm of Cranshaw, Melon and Pitts had been retained to assist. Sign here.

Without being invited to, I sat and read what I was expected to sign. The terms of my disemployment were as she had read them to me. The other paragraphs on the page absolved the firm from any responsibility for having ruined my life. I began to feel a shortness of breath. If I dropped dead without signing, I wondered, would the firm then be responsible? I felt like asking her and thought better of it. What I did ask was what would happen if I didn't sign. She referred to her instruction sheet. Anyone refusing to sign (I wondered just how many of us there were) would receive two weeks' vacation, and two weeks' severance. Some choice. Unable to help myself, (all those years of editing instructional material took control) I crossed out the 'a' before 'reorganization,' since a noun that cannot be divided does not get a modifier. Then, I signed.

I found that my humiliation was just beginning. Once again she referred to her instruction sheet. As a matter of security, she read, I was to leave the building immediately and was not to return to my office. I would, however, be allowed admittance to the fourth floor office space specifically assigned to the use of excessed personnel. That did it.

"Young lady," I said, "I would address you by name, but we have not been introduced. In the fifteen years I have been working here, a number of personal items have made their way into my office. I expect to leave with them. I also expect to leave with samples of my work. Since they contain no trade secrets and have already been distributed, there is no security problem. In fact, if I know any trade secrets, it's because I invented them and will take them with me between my ears. Have a nice day."

The long walk back to my office was made even longer by the looks I got from the other people in our department—some of whom reported to me—or used to. Nobody said a word. How did they find out? Did everyone know but me? I couldn't ask my boss because he wasn't there. So rather than think about it, I busied myself loading an empty file box with the usual detritus of an office life—the family pics, the odds and ends of old meds and the rest of the junk that is accumulated during a period of occupation at an occupation.

But after packing, what do I do? Call home? My wife was at work. One daughter was away at Tufts and thinking of law school afterward. The other was knee-deep in college catalogs. How do I word the announcement? How are we going to reconcile the bank balance with the bills?

Fifteen weeks at full pay sounds more like a golden handshake than a fickle finger. But then there were my personal demographics. Pushing fifty, I was, chronologically speaking, well into the danger zone. The last time I had changed jobs I was thirty-five. Looking at her picture reminded me that, just the other night, Cheryl and I had been discussing the financial needs of two kids in college at the same time. With both of us working, it seemed practical, despite the telephone number figure we had paid for the house when we decided the girls needed separate rooms.

I had an idea of what she would say when I told her—the same thing I was trying to tell myself: "You started your career as a Peace Corps volunteer, then as a social worker toiling in the vineyard of forgotten neighborhoods. When you chose the wife-and-family route, you literally re-engineered yourself to meet the needs of the corporate world, and worked your way up to Deputy Director of Education for a major telecommunications company. Not too shabby. This proves you're not only a fast learner, but energetic and, above all, flexible. Don't worry. You'll use these same talents to land another job."

Sure I would—once I overcame the deficits of a really weird resume, an absolute abhorrence of interviews (even when I was conducting them) and a total inability to talk about myself with the kind of enthusiasm some decision-maker would expect. And that didn't even include the current economic situation. Because one thing was certain. No matter which side of the political aisle I favored, the sad fact is that current economic policies have screwed me. More jobs have disappeared than this economy will be able to generate—at least in my working lifetime. The question I kept asking myself was: "How can someone like me compete for the jobs that are left?" Frankly, I didn't think much of my chances, but what alternative did I have? In my situation, I had no choice but to learn how.

I found out right away that there is no good way to tell people you've been fired. The play-by-play I gave Cheryl that evening got me her sympathy, but I found the questions she asked impossible to answer: "Why weren't you more alert to what was happening?" "Why wouldn't the reorganization need your talents?" "Why didn't you go over your boss' head? Haven't you been there longer than he has?"

Part 2:
Anxiety is contagious, and its symptom is anger.

It took me about a week for the shock to wear off, and then there it was. After all that time of doing good work, getting praises and raises and a reputation—even among the younger members of the staff—of being a 'can do' guy, I was out on my ass. And it wasn't just the spouse/mortgage/tuition problems that had my hand trembling as I shaved in the morning, it was because the 'why me' anger had increased to include the 'why them'? Why did they—and I mean just about everyone—behave so badly toward me? This feeling wasn't just my paranoia. All of us assembled in that church basement seemed to react the same way when the facilitator talked about anger. Perhaps that's why she encouraged us to make a list of all the 'thems' we were angry at. Here's mine. (How does it compare with yours?)

1. My boss. You'd think that with the number of times I saved his ass he could have gone to bat for me and saved mine. Or, at the very least, he could have given me a heads up. Then the way he disappeared so that he wasn't even around to say goodbye. If I didn't need his reference, I'm not sure what I would have said or done.

2. My firm. That 'reorganization' bit was just so many buffalo bagels. You don't work in one place as long as I have without building some kind of a network that would give me the real skinny. It took me just a few hours to find out that the guy they moved into my job is half my age and probably making half my salary.

3. The law. I thought perhaps I shouldn't have signed that paper until I had talked to my attorney. When I did, he reassured me by telling me I wouldn't have had a prayer. He had heard the same story from a lot of people, and he had told them all the same thing: take whatever money they offer and run.

4

Sure, from the sound of it, I was being screwed. But to get back at them, I would need a shark of a litigator. That kind of talent costs. I would have to bring an equal opportunity case, which would need a paper trail, a ton of witnesses and possibly years of time. And if I won my job back, would that be what I wanted? And punitive damages? Hard to prove and even harder to collect.

4. The whole idea of outplacement. To me, as generous as it sounds, this is a Band-aid on the company conscience. Who's kidding who? Cranshaw Melon and Pitts got the contract on a competitive bid. To make money, they've got to do as much as they can as fast as they can and move on. Those of us in my age and wage category are tough sells. We know it and they know it. So we get the resume routine: write it, send it to companies just like ours who are also cutting back and wait for lightening to strike. Fat chance. A million resumes are mailed and emailed every morning. The lottery is more certain.

5. The group. I guess a church is a logical place for confession, even if it is the basement. But what I hear scares me to death. Those who have been techies of one kind or another and have been out the longest, relate the kind of treatment they get at headhunters and agencies. It seems the longer you've been out, the further these job-finders feel you've slipped from the cutting edge. Those among us who are older don't even get interviews—except as a favor from a friend. And that kind of obligatory conversation is just that: an obligation. The facilitator tries to keep everyone thinking positive, but whom is she kidding?

6. Potential employers. During the first six weeks I've sent out more than a hundred resumes and posted myself on every job site I could find, and you know how many interviews I've had to date? None. *Somebody* has to need what I can do.

Part 3:
Putting my anger to work.

The first thing we were taught in those group sessions was to put our anger behind us. So I did. Or, at least I tried. Whenever I found myself getting into one of those 'what-I-shoulda-done' or 'what-I-shoulda-said' situations—you know the kind—complete with imaginary dialogue or visions of vengeance—I suppressed it. I kept repeating the class slogan: "Don't get angry, get started." But that was just the problem: I couldn't get started. I found that suppression led to depression. I felt so angry, that trying not to feel angry made me feel nothing at all. Defeated before I started, I couldn't generate the energy or optimism to get my show on the road.

So I switched. I began to see my anger as one of my assets. I was entitled to feel that way because I was a loyal, hard-working and good-at-problem-solving employee who wound up holding the short end of the stick. I knew my stuff and had it together. And I still do. In fact, I'm fifteen years better at solving problems than when I started. Why can't I use these skills to think through and solve my job-getting problems? And my anger would power my engine.

Not rage. Rage is blind. As a fuel it causes false starts, backfiring and stalling out. But a well-chosen anger, properly tuned, can get you where you want to go. Any way, it did it for me. Whenever I felt anger rising, I didn't suppress it. I encouraged it, with three questions:

Who, exactly, am I angry at?

What was done or not done to cause it?

What would it take to appease it?

For example, raging at my boss was easy. Letting me go may not have started life as his idea, but he probably didn't put up much of a fight. I was there when he came aboard four years ago. At the time, some people wondered—and that included me—why I had been passed over when my old boss left. Why did the firm go outside when old, faithful me was right on the spot? Was he afraid that, one day, they would start wondering the same thing?

He's not big on passing out the blue ribbons. I've been with him at meetings when someone from the carpeted floors gave one of our projects a real attaboy. He graciously accepted the praise—all the praise—as if the rest of us weren't there. Especially me. .

He's the big 'I.' Never has the first person singular been used with such consistency, or with such effect. I have never been any good at blowing my own horn. I admit it. He, on the other hand, could create a symphony with one blast of hot air.

OK, I'm sore as hell at him. And the way he behaved made it even worse. But what would it take to appease me? What do I want to salvage out of this? That's easy to answer. I want a strong letter of recommendation. Not just one of those verification-of-employment-from-this-date-to-that-date kind of thing. I've seen them, and they're about as useful as breasts on a bull. What I wanted was a letter that acknowledged some accomplishment that I was proud of having achieved—one that made the department, him, and me look good.

Part 4:
Getting good letters of reference.

But how to get them? Not by blowing my top at him, certainly. Instead, I took advantage of the way he ducked out on me when he could have offered some sympathy and support—as phony as it would have been. Since it was clear that he preferred not to get involved with me on a face-to-face basis, I wrote the letter of reference myself, and e-mailed it to him with the following note:

> *Sorry we missed each other. I figured you were busy. That's why I took the liberty of writing this suggested letter of recommendation. Could you take just a few moments to review it, print it out on letterhead, sign it and send it to me? The sooner the better. It's a tough job market out there.*

To whom it may concern:

David Abel's chief value to our organization is his ability to take the initiative in seeking the best approach to solving a problem, such as training and motivating our 24 regional management teams to submit more timely and accurate performance reports. These had to be easily accessible to corporate management personnel located in 6 headquarters worldwide.

He scoped out the project, defined the obstacles standing in the way of success and organized a team effort to overcome them. The data he gathered showed that, to achieve compliance from field personnel who were already 'too busy', our program would not only have to be implemented without down-time, but would have to include special training for corporate management in the use of this data to improve individual performance.

To achieve these objectives on budget and on time, David and his staff designed and implemented secure and restricted pages on the corporate website. The regional managers' page prompted for and accepted submissions of reports using an Excel spreadsheet template that was designed to facilitate entering complete and accurate data. A Visual Basic application at Central MIS checked them for accuracy, integrated them into a SQL Server database and returned them to the senders, along with any that might require corrections. Not only did the accuracy level jump by more than half, but the compliance rate among regional managers improved from 71% to near 100%.

We have valued David's ability to combine creativity, organizational skills, and technical facility in team efforts. He did well for us. He will do well for you.

Signed

In writing the letter I was careful, despite my anger, not to go over the top. No comparatives, for example—no terms like 'best' or 'outstanding.' I took no chance that he would dump the whole idea, and it paid off. Happy to be rid of me, I got the letter back, signed and sealed.

I *did* credit my boss with having more of an appreciation of my skills than he had ever communicated to me. But you know what? Putting those words in his mouth—every one of them the truth—made me feel better about myself than I had in weeks. It was, in fact, the first time I had really evaluated my own skills by putting them on the record. Here's what I got from the letter I had written about me:

Good at learning: Not just fast, but thorough.

Knowledgeable: user of Microsoft office application (especially Word, Excel, Frontpage) expert with Active Server Pages, SQL, VB Script to name just the headliners

Effective communicator: Trained to perceive and deal with the wants and needs of the other parties in the communication.

Skilled researcher: Whether the sought-after information was buried in text or in people.

Respecter of budgets: Like deadlines, they were established for a reason.

Flexible: The ability to change course when necessary.

Effective problem solver: Thanks to that flexibility.

Strong design and implementation skills: And a track record to prove it.

I had a lot to offer—a lot more than would fit in one letter. So, I wrote another. And then, another. It wasn't as hard as it sounds. Once I had a sample outline, all I had to do was fill in with an account of another achievement. And in the course of fifteen years, I had quite a few.

As a Deputy Director of Education he was

responsible for
in charge of
asked to solve the problem of
given the assignment of
worked with _____ in order to
worked for _____ with the responsibility to

To achieve the desired result, he:
designed a
organized a series of experiments that
managed a team of
developed a system for
created a method of
had to learn
established a procedure that

Here's how his (method) (system) (experiment) (procedure) worked: What he did first: (Drew up a plan, wrote specifications, conducted research, planned budget, established time frame, organized team)

What he did next: (Built model, tested various approaches, established assignments, monitored results)
 What next
 And so on

Here are some of the problems encountered, and how he helped to solve them:
Problem—solution

Here are the results:
 (Production) (efficiency) was improved by
 (Man-hours) (costs) were reduced by
 (Error factors went down by
 (Income) (profit) was increased by

Part 5:
Learning how to blow my horn.

As I have already made clear, self-promotion is not really my thing. I find it difficult, if not downright embarrassing, to talk about myself, much less to write it down. Perhaps, if that weren't the case, I'd still have my job. But the feeling that I was using my anger to literally force my boss to finally give me the recognition I deserved, made it easy. As I wrote, I thought, "Here's what he should have said, dammit!"

Of course there was no guarantee that he'd follow through on his end. I had the sense that a certain amount of guilt would be working for me, and that I'd get his cooperation on a glad-to-be-rid-of-the-whole-thing basis. Sure enough, a week went by and there it was. But why stop there? I still had enough anger, so I sent him another letter:

> *Thanks for your prompt response. There's always the possibility that some potential employers would value management skills over technical ability. That's why I took the liberty of writing yet another suggested letter of recommendation. Could you take just a few moments to review this one as well, print it out on letterhead, sign it and send it to me? That way I'd be able to use whichever seemed most appropriate. Thanks for your help.*

To whom it may concern:

David Abel's value to our organization is in the way he listens, records and responds to management needs. For example, downtime and discontent on the part of the customers of our telecommunication systems were making us vulnerable to competition.

In response to management's briefing, David made an analysis of customer feedback that showed not enough use was being made of the material we had gone to significant expense to provide. He felt that while our field personnel could be of some help, a faster and more cost-effective solution would be, as he termed it, 'to go direct.'

To achieve this objective, David and his team developed what they called a 'Know-How Contest' to locate and reward the most knowledgeable telecommunications personnel among our users. The contest theme: 'All you have to do to win is look it up!' motivated a closer study of our material. Weekly analysis of the scores and results not only helped to choose the winners, but showed where some of the technical information needed further clarification.

Regular status reports were sent to our field personnel so that they would be in a position to encourage and improve accuracy.

As a result, during the first six months of the new program, questions and calls for technical backup from participating customers were reduced by more than one half. We have valued David's ability to combine creativity, organizational skills, and managerial understanding in team efforts. He did well for us. He will do well for you.

Signed

To my list of assets I was able to add:

Determined note-taker: A believer in the idea that your memory is not your friend and can betray you at any time.

Highly accurate: Producing wanted results—largely due to accurate note taking at meetings and assignment sessions.

Experienced organizer: The ability to see the project as a whole, as well as each of its parts.

Respecter of deadlines: Each project has a beginning, middle, and an end. Each stage has a date, which was established for a purpose.

I realized I was having fun doing this. What you're seeing, of course, is the final product. I had to do a lot of cutting, so that it read quickly and focused my story. You know why? Because once the account of my achievement began to take shape, there was a big temptation to run off at the mouth. I caught myself including a whole lot of 'and besides that....' kind of stuff that clogged the arteries of my story. I'm an educator. Keeping things simple and easy to understand is my discipline. So that's what I did.

The fun came from putting it to my boss. Or should I be referring to him as my ex-boss by now? This way of letting him know what he had let go was the most productive use of anger I could imagine. And having that first letter signed and returned was the most productive result. Of course, I didn't have much hope of seeing the others.

Others? Yes, others! Why not? Every time I came up with a new letter, I sent it to him. My thinking was that unless I heard anything to the contrary, what I was saying was right, and right on point and I could use it. Besides, this was good therapy for me. Each time I wrote one of those letters, I became more and more convinced that my assets outweighed my liabilities. Yes, I had liabilities, which would have been foolish to deny:

Not very good at selling myself: No matter how hard I try, I just can't blow my own horn as loud as it seems to take.

Slow verbal response: I prefer to think carefully about how I want to answer a question, perhaps even refer to my notes. This could make some listeners impatient.

Loose fit in the corporate structure: I can do everything from designing the approach, creating the material, and administering the project. I run the risk of being ruled out as too heavy for light work and too light for heavy work.

Age: When I was hiring I have to admit I preferred younger people.

Detest interviews: Not just because I don't like telling strangers about myself, but because of the feeling I'm pretending to be somebody else.

Out of practice: Haven't looked for a job in 15 years.

Uncertain about which approach to use: headhunter, career services, want ads, do-it-myself, which?

Depressed and anxious: A bad place from which to start.

Part 6:
It helps to get angry at—yourself.

For six weeks I shared the experiences and attitudes of everyone else in the room. We all railed against supposed friends who had turned their backs, brushed us off with promises of a lunch 'sometime,' or asked for a resume with which they did nothing. The same went for potential employers to whom we sent great cover letters and resumes (we exchanged and reviewed them) and got no response. Secretaries, assistants and phone-mail came in for their share of the blame. We were loud, we were angry—and we were wrong. And it took those six precious weeks for me to realize it.

It happened by accident. Hoping to start some up-beat discussion going, I explained how I had gone about getting my letter of recommendation. I thought it was a pretty neat thing—using my anger against my ex-boss to generate some positive thoughts about myself—and getting the evidence to prove it at an interview. That was when the roof fell in. "If you're such a great problem-solver," somebody asked, "how come you're still here?"

While I was trying to come up with an answer, our facilitator reminded us that we were to avoid challenge and criticism and the incident was passed over. But, not for me. Whoever said it was dead right. I *was* a problem-solver. I have the ability to study a situation and find the key that unlocks the door to the objective. The letter said as much. But I was at the wrong door. What was the point of preparing for the interview unless I could solve the problem of *getting* an interview? Pretty obvious, wasn't it? So I turned my anger toward myself:

1. Why did I wait this long to evaluate my skills and develop a dossier of successes? I refer, not just to these past weeks, but these past years. If I had started this kind of thinking years ago, I might have been in a stronger position to interview for the top spot when my old boss left. They still might have gone outside, but I would have had a shot at making a more positive impression than the one they obviously shared.

2. Why did I ignore the message my company was sending me? Was it that I just didn't want to hear it? Was I convinced that they were right when they passed me over? That would have been a great time to re-evaluate my accomplishments and test the open market. That would have been a great time to listen to those siren calls about, "Hey, if you're ever planning to leave your present spot, we're interested." If nothing else, I might have honed the rust off my job-getting skills.

3. Why did I ever take my employment for granted? Comfort? Security? Retirement? Forget it. The current corporate idea of the best way to lighten the ship during the storm is to throw the crew overboard. And the day of the golden handshake? Only for the top guys—the people who had flushed the company down the toilet in the first place. So instead of looking for a job that would bind my fate to that of a single organization, I'll look for *work*: work that makes the best use of my skills at the best possible price to whoever is ready to pay it.

4. Why didn't I wait until I had a clear idea of what I had to offer and where my skills would find the best possible application? Without any kind of thought or preparation, I immediately contacted everybody on my Rolodex and sent resumes to the key firms in my industry. Bad, bad, bad idea. I was totally disorganized. I must have sounded like I was frantic and begging. They reacted like I was contagious. A waste of time. And a waste of what I thought were good contacts.

Now that I had identified the target of my anger and the reason for it, what it would take to appease it was fairly obvious. I have these skills to sell. Who would need them enough to want to buy them—not just in telecommunications, but anywhere at all? What I needed were more than contacts. I needed guides, mentors, coaches, advisors, tutors, teachers, gurus. I needed people who could read one or even more of my paragraphs, understand the value of what I was offering, and *want* to tell me they'd like to discuss it further.

Part 7:
How I found the people I needed.

What I found in my search was that the cliché is true: every business *is* different. While there are some common denominators that apply to broad categories of enterprise: profit vs. non-profit, manufacturing vs. distributing, commercial vs. academic, service vs. product, etc., there are significant differences in trade language, customs and the structure of the decision-making ladder. My first rule of thumb was to try like crazy to resist any preconceived notions of what I thought I knew. I had to behave like what I really was—a foreigner. Instead of guidebooks, dictionaries, and a few restaurant recommendations, I needed company literature, articles in the business press or trade journals, and some recommendations of whom to approach.

Fortunately, every industry worthy of the name has a trade press. Even more fortunately, the publications were either on the shelves in the business section of my library or at the other end of my favorite search engines. Maybe it wasn't the greatest leisure reading experience of my life, but each article gave me an insight into the customs and language of yet another business environment by answering the following questions:

What do they call the people who buy from them?

Customers, Franchisees, Dealers, Owners, Independent Operators, Retailers, Distributors, Installers, Service Outlets?

Through whom do they deal with the people who buy from them?

Direct, Distributors, Factory Reps, Area Managers, Regional Warehouse, Sales Staff?

How do they communicate with the people who buy from them?

Catalogues, Specification Books, Service Manuals, Price Lists, Computer Network, Trade Shows, Sales Meetings, Personal Reps?

How's business?

Expanding because of current market opportunities? Hurting, because of costly administrative problems? Surviving, despite severe competition?

I didn't have to learn everything there was to know. To the contrary, my lack of knowledge of these other fields and where my skills would fit were the reasons why I needed guides, mentors, coaches, etc. All I really had to have, going in, was enough knowledge of the language and customs to understand what they were telling me.

Naturally, I tried the easy ones first. I knew some people who worked in areas I had targeted as possibilities. I had even called one or two already—which was enough to convince me that, in future, to keep my fingers off that dial. Unless we were in the habit of exchanging social chit-chat or were regulars for lunch or a few beers, my call from out of the blue would sound, and be dealt with, just like what it was: an interruption.

Instead, I began to analyze why my past approaches had failed. I'm the kind of guy who researches a problem, right? So I did some research. It was easy. I called several of the people to whom I had sent resumes but who 'didn't recall receiving them.' As I might have expected, I wound up with their administrative assistants. But this time, those were the very people I wanted to talk to.

Since I'm not the best ad-libber in the world, I prepared every word I was going to say and rehearsed them. I realized that I was going to be operating on borrowed time and that if I fumbled or was hesitant they would hang up on me.

They:	Mr. Biggs office. This is Wendy.
Me:	Wendy, this is David Abel. You may or may not recall my name, but I need a minute's worth of your advice? OK?
They:	What's this about?
Me:	I'd appreciate the answer to just one question: How do you decide which mail or phone communications get through to Mr. Bigg?
They:	I don't decide that. He does. If he doesn't know the caller or the sender, he doesn't want to be bothered. Resumes and other SPAM like that go right to HR.
Me:	Thanks a lot, Wendy. You've been very helpful.

They: I don't see how, but you're welcome

Wendy, and a few others I talked to, had two things in common. First, since all I asked for was the answer to one question, they were willing to answer. Second, they failed to recognize how helpful they had been. What they told me was a tough challenge, but not unexpected. With all those resumes in the mail or on the Internet every day, busy decision-makers were running for cover behind assistants, phone-mail and e-mail blockers. You could hate them for it, but you could hardly blame them. But by telling me what kind of communication does *not* get through, they were giving me the specs for those that would:

If he doesn't know the caller or the sender, he doesn't want to be bothered.

Understandable, if not encouraging. So whatever I send has to look personal and suggest that we know each other.

Resumes and other SPAM like that go right to HR.

This was painful, because I thought I had a pretty good resume. But it was also my cue to stay away from anything that looks like a request for a job. Even the J-word word is out. And if it looks like it's just another blanket mailing, it's SPAM.

OK, where does that leave me?

I'm contacting this person because I'm looking for a mentor who knows a particular field or industry in which I am interested. I have to make clear that I'm not looking for a job—not as a device to trick the contact into giving me the time of day—but because I believe, that in this market, JOB is a thing of the past. Job title, description and compensation are part of a company's overhead. It's a square on the organization chart that represents outgo. WORK, on the other hand, is what helps to grow the company by adding to its profit, productivity and efficiency. Instead of outgo, it's income, and what organization couldn't use more income?

Furthermore, to hire anyone these days, a company has to make a commitment: everything from retirement benefits to health insurance. Then, if it doesn't work out or there's a cutback, there's the cost of the separation. When profits were up and skilled labor harder to find, it didn't matter. Now it does. And a 50-year-old? Multiply all those considerations by a factor of who-knows-how-much.

And, from my point of view, as my recent history has proved, being tied to the fortunes of one company is no bargain. If they decide, for whatever reason, that I'm excess baggage, I'm left with nothing else. Or they have some kind of reorganization and I wind up doing work I hate. Or my boss is a horse's ass. That's why I don't want yet another job with another company. What I want is work from as many different companies as I can reach.

Why not? We're in the era of flex time and work-from-home. Outsourcing is now part of the language. And I'm not in Bangladesh, I'm right here.

According to my experience, people who have no job to offer avoid jobseekers. Why should they go out of their way to turn someone away? Unless they're sadists, disappointing people isn't much fun. But being a mentor and sharing their expertise is a whole other thing.

When I brought this idea up in group, a number of them yelled, "Networking!" What's different, they wondered, about networking? Just about everyone looking for a job has been to that well any number of times. That's why it's dried up: too many people looking for too many favors.

Favors! That's the word I jumped on. Asking someone to do me the favor of asking someone else for a favor, so that they might ask yet another someone else for a favor, is too much to expect. The very term implies that the giver is getting nothing in return. If that's the case, we're all knocking on the wrong doors. It's up to us to find people who can benefit from what we can do for *them*. And since I carry the additional burden of being older, it's up to me to be interesting enough—because of my experience in achieving success for others—to *earn* their interest in talking to me. And I have to be structured, prepared and organized to take as little of their time as possible.

Then there's the personal angle. In order to get past all the guardians, I have to know the contact, or I have to know enough about the contact to personalize my message. This sets up a sort of Contact Hierarchy:

Contacts I know personally or have met.

Contacts I may not have met personally, but have heard speak, or have read articles by or about them.

Contacts to whom I have been referred by people *they* know.

With all my findings in place, I was ready to go. After all those negative definitions of 'networking,' I planned to keep my ideas to myself for the time being, not sharing them with my fellow searchers. But I have a life partner with a vested interest. I was also a bit on the defensive, knowing that I might sound like I was giving up and joining the statistic of the tens of thousands of job-seekers who were no longer seeking. Sure enough, that was Cheryl's reaction.

It was my fault, I think. I'm afraid I gave the impression that what I found out had me beat. What I should have made clear from the outset, was that this information would serve as a guide through the minefield between my potential contacts and me. But what turned the discussion around was my analysis of the term

JOB itself. I explained that, for a middle manager, JOB was a series of projects, one after the other. Some were in response to something that was happening that top management didn't want to happen. Some were in response to something that wasn't happening that top management wanted to happen. Some results took months to achieve. Some took weeks. Some took days. My *job* was to be on hand to take on those projects. My *work* was to successfully complete each of them.

More important, each project called for a different assortment of skills. There were instances where my research abilities were the key. There were others where my training talent was most important. And still others where my management capabilities made it work. So forget titles. In this market they are meaningless, anyway. What *has* meaning is whatever result top management is after. What do they want started? What do they want stopped? Whatever it is, they can rent the result: by the month, week or day—from me. Of course if the *ideal* job opportunity did come along, I'd be a fool not to consider it, wouldn't I?

But what was out there? Was there work that I could do? Where was it? And would they prefer to rent or buy? There was only one sure way to find out: ask them. But who is them and how do I reach them? My communications would have to be personal—or *seem* personal. They would have to make clear that this was no job hunt. And one thing more: my communications would have to keep knocking until someone opened the door.

Part 8:
Developing Contact Communication.

From this line of logic came my Contact Communication. I deliberately avoided the term 'letter' because I wasn't sure what form this communication would take: a letter, a note, a memo, e-mail, whatever. To make it easy, I started with the people I knew or had met in the past. I even wrote the people who had made it clear that my unemployment was of little or no interest to them, but that I should 'keep in touch.' So I did:

Contact Communication to people I knew:

Mr. John Contact
World Technologies
123 Universe Ave.
Any City, U.S.A.

Dear John,

I know you asked me to keep in touch, but things have been pretty hectic since we last spoke. I've been busy with a research project and, to complete it, I need to meet with you long enough to ask just one question, make some notes and be on my way. Would you mind being my mentor for about 15 minutes next Thursday?

What started my thinking was a time/cost/result analysis I made of a project to train and motivate 24 regional management teams to submit more timely and accurate performance reports for 6 headquarters worldwide.

To get it done on budget and on time, my staff and I designed and implemented secure and restricted pages on the corporate website. The regional managers' page prompted for and accepted submissions of reports, using an Excel spread-sheet template that was designed to facilitate entering complete and accurate data. A Visual Basic application at Central MIS checked them for accuracy, integrated them into a SQL Server database and returned them to the senders, along with any that might require corrections. Not only did the accuracy level jump by more than half, but the compliance rate among regional managers improved from 71% to near 100%.

Now here's what I have to know, John. Suppose, instead of hiring me, would companies be ready to *rent* results like these on a monthly, weekly or even daily basis? If so, by what criteria? I'm particularly interested in those who buy or lease your equipment.

Is Thursday OK? I'll call you the day before, to set a time. If that's not convenient, will you leave word with your assistant about the best time to get together?

Thanks, John, I appreciate your guidance.
Signed

The heart of this Contact Communication was 'borrowed' from one of my letters of recommendation. (The more paragraphs I write, the more material I have for my contact campaign.) When the happy day comes that I need to show a letter of recommendation, the fact that it tells a consistent story won't hurt, either. It also saves a great deal of work.

I know you asked me to keep in touch, but things have been pretty hectic since we last spoke.

"Keep in touch" was a throwaway phrase. Everybody said "keep in touch" when what they really meant was "goodbye forever" But opening my letter that way lent a personal feeling to the communication. It was more likely to survive the scrutiny of the guardian at the gate. When John reads it, even if he doesn't remember saying it, he might well have done so.

I've been busy with a research project and, to complete it, I need to meet with you long enough to ask just one question, make some notes and be on my way.

This sentence is important for what it doesn't say. It doesn't say that I'm looking for a job. It doesn't say that I'm not looking for a job. The J-word isn't even part of the communication. This sentence is also important for what it *does* say. It says that I'm not going to ask for anything the reader can't easily give me. This means I won't be putting him on the defensive, or embarrassing him in any way. I won't even need a lot of his valuable time. One question and I'm gone. (What's the one question? Read on to find out what it's about.)

Would you mind being my mentor for about 15 minutes next Thursday?

When was the last time John was asked to be anybody's mentor? Most probably, never.

Suppose, instead of hiring me, companies could rent results like these on a monthly, weekly or even daily basis?

The line I have heard most frequently lately is, "We're not doing any hiring at present." So why fight it? There must be a lot of organizations out there that want more—more productivity, more profit, more efficiency. What they don't want is more people on their payroll. OK, then, why not rent instead of buy? It's not that radical a concept. Like I say, outsourcing is now part of the system. It's just that I've never been part of that system and therefore don't know by what criteria companies decide to outsource. Further, I don't know the inner workings of any company but my past employer. So my question has to do with the criteria.

I'm particularly interested in those who buy or lease your equipment.

Those who do business with you, BUT NOT YOUR COMPANY. At least, not necessarily—unless you're personally interested in the idea. I could also have expressed interest in companies with many branch offices, or a large field force from which they were getting poor compliance. Or with many customers using new equipment. Or with a field force that needed training. The variations would depend on what paragraph I had decided to use.

Is Thursday OK? I'll call you the day before, to set a time. If that's not convenient, will you leave word with your assistant about the best time to get together?

Here's the big difference. Instead of asking to be called, or waiting to be called, or praying to be called, I'm doing the calling.

Thanks, John, I appreciate your guidance.

And *how* I do.

How does it all add up? It sounds personal, chatty almost. I intend to use ordinary letterhead without fancy typefaces or format to avoid a resume atmosphere. And speaking of resumes, there is none attached.

I've stressed the fact there is one piece of specific information the reader has that I need. That's all I'm looking for—which is why it's OK to re-contact people who may have already brushed me off. That account of an achievement shows that I'm no lightweight. I've outlined some specific skills that make me an interesting person to see, rather than just wasting the time it takes to accommodate an acquaintance. And my promise to ask just one question, make some notes, and be on my way, means a concise and goal-oriented conversation instead of a job plea. So neither of us will need a lot of time.

I found that asking people for a job appealed to their sympathy, empathy and generosity. I was always disappointed. I figured that asking people to mentor me would appeal to their status, their expertise, and their sense of their own security. I was rarely disappointed.

I did have one concern: what I was doing wasn't at all like the usual me. I was brought up on Proverbs 27:2: "Let another man praise thee, and not thine own mouth." But that was written for another time and another world. Growing up, I was always being advised to be patient—that "All things come to those who wait." It wasn't until I grew up and read the second part of that verse that I learned they might come too late.

But the biggest adjustment was the move from passive to assertive. Not aggressive. Assertive. The former suggests a kind of 'pushyness' I could never accept in others, leastwise myself. The latter means that I know my own worth and wish others to know it as well. I was angry with 'them' for not knowing it, but the truth is that I was mainly angry with myself for keeping it a secret. In a way I was creating a new me, and at my time of life that wasn't easy. Necessary, perhaps, but not easy.

What I was doing was more work than simply answering ads or turning myself over to a head-hunter. When I found myself getting anxious, which was often, I relaxed by reviewing the common sense of what I was doing:

Personal communications that ask for a meeting to write and take a lot of work. But it's the name of the game. I found that the best way to master it was to keep it simple. Say exactly what I want right up front. Next, say exactly why I deserve to have it. Then, express my gratitude with my promise to call.

Why not just call in the first place? It's quicker, it's easier and it saves learning how to write. After all, I know John. Why not just pick up the phone and give him a ring? There are at least three reasons:

The first reason is timing. I put myself in the place of a contact who might be waiting for a call from a major customer, his boss, the hospital, his lawyer, his lover, or the doctor who performed those special tests just that morning. In other words, there is sure to be more going on between the ears of the person I was trying to reach than I could ever dream of. My call at the wrong time is an invasion.

The second reason is one of communication. A phone call out of the blue can never come across as clearly as a well planned letter. Knowing my weakness at adlibbing, I would probably say the wrong thing at the wrong time. (Not 'probably.' I usually did.)

The third reason is one of simple courtesy. My contact may have time to see me, but chances are better than even money that some times are better than others. A written communication, rather than an untimely phone call out of the blue, gives my contact more time to plan the time. If my writing makes the right impression, my contact may want to do some research on my behalf. He may even want to pass my communication around! This too, will take time.

Does this mean that I expected my Contact Communication to be an automatic door-opener? Hardly. But I planned to keep sending one after another until that door *did* open. What I wanted were CC's that worked, and if the first one didn't, the next might. And if that didn't, the next one might. And so on. I expected to be angry with people who did not respond. All I had to do was forge that anger into determination.

Part 9:
Finding contacts at job fairs.

This meant that I would also need to contact people I didn't know. So I made yet another big adjustment: two, in fact. For one thing, I'm not all that good at glad-handing…those mob venues at meetings and conventions where you're supposed to ease up to some total stranger, squint at their lapel badge, introduce yourself and start a conversation. But I had to find the people, so I had to develop a strategy I could live with.

I ran off some business cards on my PC. Nothing fancy, just the necessary information. But, under my name, I put the phrase, *"RENT RESULTS, INC."* The card really wasn't meant to be read as much as swapped. I launched the idea at one of those job fairs. You know the kind, where everybody is wandering from booth to booth delivering their resume from a stack they brought along for the purpose. Maybe doing that wasn't a bad idea, but that wouldn't serve my purpose. I needed the names of people and companies I could research. Then I could use our meeting as the basis for a personal approach.

No big deal. I walked up to somebody, stuck out my hand and said my name. They said theirs. I handed them my card. They handed me theirs. Instead of giving them a resume, I took out a small notebook:

Me: Tell me, Mr./Ms/how does Whatsis International make productive use of the data it collects?

Sometimes I got a response, which I noted in my pad, next to the name. Sometimes I got a confused look and was handed a company brochure from a stack on the table. But SOMETIMES, if my luck was running, I got the admission that the person at the booth was not that high up on the food chain, (which is why he was stuck with that chore in the first place!) and that the person to see was……. No, that person wasn't at the fair, but I can reach him/her by contacting……. I thanked them profusely, made a note in my book and moved on. In my head was the new opening paragraph for my letter:

Fred Friendly
VP, Operations,
Whatsis International
Anywhere, USA

Dear Fred,

When Charlie Smith and I were talking the other day, he told me that if anyone in your organization knew how Whatsis International makes use of its data it would be Fred Friendly. So here I am. I've been busy with a research project and, to complete it, I need to meet with you long enough to ask just one question, make some notes and be on my way. Would you mind being my mentor for about 15 minutes next Thursday?

(The balance of my letter was the same as the example already shown.)

Just for the fun of it, I sprang that opening paragraph on the gang in the basement. (Actually, I didn't do it for fun. Down deep I was still curdled about those sarcastic remarks concerning my problem-solving skills and wanted to prove I still had it when it counted.) Of course, I made sure to wait until it had all worked out and I had already been through a productive session with Fred Friendly. That way, I was ready to respond to any comments or questions:

Q:	How could you lie like that?
A:	Sorry, but what about that paragraph is untrue? Charlie Smith was manning the booth at a job fair when I introduced myself. We talked. I asked him how Whatsis International makes use of its data. He didn't know. I asked him who *would* know. He told me it would be Fred Friendly. How is any of that untrue?
Q:	OK, it wasn't a lie. But you didn't know Fred Friendly well enough to address him by his first name, and your letter gives the impression that you did.
A:	Darn right. But how else could I be sure he even got to see my letter? Besides, these days, a lot of people use your first name even when they don't know you. Call a rental car company. Call your PC service desk. It's sup-

posed to be informal and friendly. Well, that's what I want to be—informal and friendly.

Q: What happened when you met? Did he bring that up?

A: He never mentioned it. The only reference he made to my letter was to ask me about the one question I was going to ask. That had him intrigued.

Part 10:
Finding contacts at trade shows

Job fairs are pretty good places to make contacts, but trade shows are even better. If I read about a trade show in town that interested me, I'd go. Not first thing, during the time when I'd have to register and possibly be denied admittance, but later in the morning when lots of people are moving around. I carried an official-looking folder, which gave me license to read the signs listing the seminars and their speakers. During the usual milling around the entryway before the session started, it was card-swapping and name-taking time. This time my question was:

Me: Hi, I'm Dave Abel. What interests you in this particular workshop, may I ask?

I made a discovery. Asking the first question works like a pre-emptive strike. By asking the question up front, I put my new acquaintance at ease. I wasn't selling anything or coming up with any surprises. What I wanted to talk about was an interest we obviously shared, since we were at the same seminar. I also got a name and a business card in response to offering mine.

Most important, I also got answers (which I noted) and no one asked *me* anything: not even why I was asking questions! I couldn't help wondering what I would have told them if they had. How would it have sounded if I had said, "I'm just collecting names so I can begin my letter with a paragraph like this?

Mr. John Contact
World Technologies
123 Universe Ave.
Any City, U.S.A.

Dear John,

When our conversation was interrupted last Friday at the Hotel Management Convention, you were telling me your ideas about motivating change through the collection of accurate and timely data. From what you shared with me, you may be the very mentor I'm looking for. Could I meet with you long enough to ask just one question, make some notes and be on my way? Could you spend 15 minutes next Thursday?

While the basic letter was the same, I began with a brief reference to the ideas that passed between us. I figured that my contact probably wouldn't remember. These affairs are like cocktail parties where people meet, chat and move on. (This also means that the sooner I wrote after we had met the better for me.)

Part 11:
Finding contacts through the trade press.

Another big adjustment I had to make was my negative attitude toward trade press. I felt it was more PR than real news. But when I focused my attention on specific organizations or industries, I wasn't looking for news. I was looking for names. I made note of those names and notes of the quotes. And if an entire article was authored by some authority in the business, I made a copy I could quote from. Since I had never met this contact, how was I to address him/her? People who get quoted in the trade press are generally important enough to be hard to reach. Would a positive comment on the article be personal enough to get by the guardians at the gate? Or would a first-name-basis be the key? It would cost 37 cents to find out.

First, I tried the standard approach:

Mr. Charles Smith
Vice President, Marketing
Acme Auto Parts, Inc
Anywhere, USA

Dear Mr. Smith,

Your talk, "Merchandising Auto Parts for the Upscale Market" at the Denver meeting as reported in the June issue of AFTERMARKET MAGAZINE was very informative. But since my expertise is data management, not aftermarket, it got me to wondering. How does your industry gather, monitor and use the data to motivate the "corrections upward or downward" that you referred to?

I'm presently in the midst of a data time/cost/result analysis project and, to complete it, I need to meet with someone with your ideas just long enough to ask just one question make some notes and be on my way. Would you mind being my mentor for about 15 minutes next Thursday?

What encouraged me to contact you was the similarity in our approach to problem solving…

Sounds good? I thought so. But when I made my follow-up call, nyet. They never got my letter—which means I never got through. My communication had been round-filed or was on its way to HR. Was I angry and discouraged? I was angry, but not discouraged. It was a what-have-I-got-to-lose kind of anger that sent this one to the *same* contact:

Mr. Charles Smith
Vice President, Marketing
Acme Auto Parts, Inc
Anywhere, USA

Dear Charlie,

Your talk, "Merchandising Auto Parts for the Upscale Market" at the Denver meeting had the audience taking notes, which in my experience is a real first at sessions like these. I think everyone found your information to be informative and well-presented. But since my expertise is data management, not aftermarket, it got me to wondering. How does your industry gather, monitor and use the data to motivate the "corrections upward or downward" that you referred to?

I'm presently in the midst of a data time/cost/result analysis project and, to complete it, I need to meet with someone with your ideas just long enough to ask just one question make some notes and be on my way. Would you mind being my mentor for about 15 minutes next Thursday?

What encouraged me to contact you was the similarity in our approach to problem solving….

I didn't have to bring this one to the group to know what their reaction would be. It made me nervous just to write something like that. While everything was true and taken from the article, the implication that I was present at the meeting itself and may have had enough communication with Mr. Smith to address him as 'Charlie' was just that—an implication. But my reasoning was basic: what did I have to lose? The more formal approach—OK, the more *factual* approach—had already failed. Besides, when Charlie agreed to see me, it was because of what I said in the body of my letter. If that hadn't been of any interest, whether I had actually been at the meeting or not would have been of little consequence.

But since my expertise is data management, not aftermarket, it got me to wondering. How does your industry gather and monitor the data needed to make the "corrections upward or downward" that you referred to?

Finding a specific reference is what good research is all about. Quoting it is even better. And, as I have found throughout my working life, good research leads to more research. How *does* the aftermarket industry in general or this organization in particular gather and monitor its data? After all, my expertise (in this case) is data management, not aftermarket, so it's a logical question for me to ask.

I'm presently in the midst of a data time/cost/result analysis project and, to complete it, I need to meet with someone with your ideas just long enough to ask just one question make some notes and be on my way.

This sentence gives me a reason for being at the conference, as well as letting the contact know that I, too, am in the midst of something and that my time, too, is valuable.

The central problem was still getting through to the individual with whom I wanted to meet. If one format—a letter, for example—didn't work, how about other kinds of communication that Might land on the contact's desk?

How about an Interoffice Memo?

Interoffice Memos could be sent snail mail, e-mail, FAX or hand delivery. The personal link with the Contact was only one way of separating this communication from the rain of resumes and SPAM directed toward him/her every day. But there was also the language. I borrowed the achievement from the letter format, but the telegram-type sentence structure made it sound different:

7/27/03
TO: John Contact
FROM: David Abel
SUBJECT: Conversation at Hotel Management Convention, 7/26/03

1. Topic of conversation: motivating change through the collection of accurate and timely data. From ideas you shared, you may be the very mentor I'm searching for. Could we meet long enough for just one question and some note-taking? 15 minutes some time next Thursday, perhaps?

2. Encouraged to contact you due to similarity in our approach to problem solving. To cite example, my objective was to train and motivate 24

regional management teams to submit more timely and accurate performance reports to be accessible to corporate management located in 6 headquarters worldwide. Research indicated compliance from field personnel would not only have to be implemented without down-time, but would have to include training for corporate management in the use of data as constructive guide for improving individual performance.

3. To achieve objectives: designed and implemented secure and restricted pages on corporate website. Web page created for regional managers prompted for and accepted submissions of regional reports using Excel spreadsheet template designed to facilitate entering complete and accurate data. Spreadsheets emailed to Central MIS where Visual Basic application checked them for accuracy. Those passing test were integrated into SQL Server database and returned by e-mail acknowledgments to senders, along with any requiring corrections.

4. Results: accuracy level jumped by more than half, and compliance rate among regional managers improved from 71% to near 100%.

5. Question: would companies in your industry be interested in *renting* results like these on a monthly, weekly or even daily basis? By what criteria would they decide?

6. Question: Is Thursday OK? Will call the day before to set a time. If not convenient, will you leave word with your assistant about the best time to get together?

The big advantage of the memo format was that it could be sent any number of ways—including personal delivery in one of those interoffice manila jobs. What the heck—if it was in the city, I didn't mind playing 'messenger service' for a few hours. Like the other Contact Communication, all I was asking for was a conversation. Not simply a friendly chat, however, but a *Contact* Conversation, focused on my question. Not a Job Interview with its attendant stress on both parties, but a pair of professionals meeting in a relaxed, mentor-learner relationship.

No matter what response I got, (outside of 'yes,' of course) I was prepared to keep right on asking. Sure I got discouraged and I got angry. Being ignored or rejected isn't the best feeling in the world. But I was supposed to be a problem-solver and this was just one more problem to solve.

Part 12:
Making the Follow-up Call.

Now this was the sticky part. My Contact Communications, as effective as I could make them, didn't actually make the contact. I had to do that. That's why I asked for permission to call:

Is Thursday OK? I'll call you the day before to set a time. If that's not convenient, will you leave word with your assistant about the best time to get together?

My reason was not only to alert the contact that I was going to call, but also to give me something personal to say to the Guardian at the Gate, whoever that might be. The script I prepared—because I knew I could never do it all adlib—went like this:

They:	Mr. Contact's office. This is Wendy,
Me:	Hi, Wendy, this is David…David Abel. I promised him I'd call today.

By not referring to my contact as Mr. or Ms. I hoped to keep everything kind of informal and maintain the personal touch that I had been warned about. (If it sounded like the contact and I were total strangers, I would be dead.). I also discovered that if I sounded at all hesitant and uncertain, the Guardian would sense that, and the next thing I would hear was the what-is-this-in-reference-to beginning of the end. So I rehearsed, until I felt I had allowed just the right time interval between saying my first name and then my full name.

I did not ask if my contact was available. While I didn't expect to convey the impression that he was sitting there just waiting for my call, I didn't want to invite excuses, either. The fact that *I promised him I'd call today* was the absolute truth. For all I knew, he was intrigued by my communication and interested in talking to me. Here I was, living up to my promise to call.

The idea of keeping the conversation on a familiar, first-name basis may not have been important, but I was trying to avoid that awful question about what my call was in reference to—and for the most part, I did. And for the most part, the guardians and I had friendly, intelligent conversations.

The friendliest and most intelligent, of course, was when I was connected to the contact to find that he/she had read my Communication and was ready to set up an appointment. But there were others

My contact read my Communication, was willing to provide the information I needed, but was too busy to set up an appointment right now.

My contact read my Communication but felt he or she was the wrong person to give me information I needed.

My contact read my Communication, did not wish to get involved, and wanted to dispose of me as quickly as possible.

My contact did not read my Communication and does not even remember receiving it.

The negatives, of course, outweighed the positives. I expected as much. I used to be an optimist, but those first six weeks had made me a realist. That's why I got ready to deal with each situation before I made the follow-up call.

I had to consider the number of people—including myself—who may have asked these same contacts to help them locate a job. I had to consider the number of people—including myself—who may have pretended to be asking these same contacts for information, but wound up asking for a job. If they had no jobs to offer, this past experience was going to make some of those contacts gun-shy enough to want to avoid involvement in my needs.

It isn't fair. Most of us, at one time or another, have encountered a mentor who played a vital role in our lives. Maybe it was a teacher, a colleague, or a boss whose help was accepted. You would think that, based on the principle that help accepted is an obligation to pass it on, we would all be more supportive of each other. But who said life was fair? So, I welcomed the best, but prepared for the worst. For example, maybe my contact had left word.

They:	Mr. Contact's office. This is Wendy.
Me:	Hi, Wendy, this is David…David Abel. I promised him I'd call today.
They:	He's in, but he's at a meeting.
Me:	By any chance did he leave word about the best time for us to get together?
They:	Let me check his appointments. (Pause) Yes, he has you on his screen for Friday, the 9th, at 2:00:

Me: Thanks, Wendy. Friday the 9th at 2:00 sounds good. I look forward to seeing you.

This is not la-la-land and not everything I sent worked that well. I've had contacts answer their own phone, tell me they read what I had sent but were too busy to see me right now. Why don't I call again on Monday? And I believed them, until Monday. Then, either a Guardian or phone-mail screened me out. I had to learn to get ready for that one:

They: I'm too busy to see you right now.

Me: It sounds like there could be a possible time crunch during the week ahead, and that you're too nice a person to make a date and then stand me up. I really appreciate that. But speaking for myself, I only need fifteen minutes—and I'm more than willing to come to your office and wait for an opening. No obligation. And if there is any industry literature you could leave for me to study while I'm waiting, that would be a real help all in itself. Is there any morning or afternoon that offers the best chance?

Without working out a script in advance, I'd have been lost. I think most people would. We're on the phone and we can't see each other, so the words are everything. Well, not quite everything. Taking the time to think about what my contact may be thinking and preparing for it, helped me to avoid a fast-talking, high-volume speech pattern that could sound like high pressure when it was really just my panic.

They: Why don't you call me sometime later in the month?

In the technical language of communication, I found that this was called an 'oh-oh.' My contact is interested enough to see me, but not willing to set aside a major project, divorce proceeding, business trip, elective surgery or vacation. But as in the previous situation, I only wanted that same 15 minutes:

Me: It sounds like there could be a possible time crunch during the weeks ahead, Mr. Contact, and that you're too nice a person to make a date and then stand me up. I really appreciate that. Would contacting you on the 21st be a better time? Or would the 28th be even better?

They:	The 28th, I think.
Me:	Great! Would you have any industry literature I might study in the meantime? If you could leave it for me with someone I'll be happy to come by tomorrow and pick it up. I would be most grateful, and whatever time you could spare me would be far more productive. Whom should I ask for?
They:	I'll have my secretary leave it at reception.
Me:	Thanks. If you could mark it for David Abel, that's A-b-e-l, I'd appreciate it.

The field reps in my old outfit used to talk about 'keeping the deal green.' What they meant was never really taking a 'no' as an end to the communication. The fact that my Contact can't see me and doesn't even want me to call for the next two weeks could be a brush-off. Or, it could be true that he'll be away for a while. If he left the material at the reception desk and marked for me, that's a positive sign. If not, it could be bad news. Or, it could mean my Contact simply forgot. Or the person to whom the job was delegated forgot. But in any case, *I'm on the premises.* I can say with all honesty that Mr. Contact told me to come by and that the material would be at reception. If I can get word to him that I'm there, I might get more than the material I'm after. Stranger things happened.

While the best deal from my point of view was face to face, this wasn't always possible. So I was ready with my 'telephone offer:'

Me:	A 15-minute telephone chat would give me the help I need, Mr. Contact. I know it's crazy to ask a busy person like yourself when you plan not to be busy, but would day or evening be more likely?

If my contact was an earlier-than-anybody bird, I got some pre-business hour. More than once I got the home number—if I promised to keep to the fifteen minutes. I would promise—with a reminder to the contact to keep my letter handy. It would save time.

During my calls, I kept one thought in mind: how different is this from making a date with a friend? Not everybody runs on the same timetable. Many social and business meetings are a matter of negotiating the best time for all concerned. However, if I was anxious—and my anxiety showed—I could tell that it was making people nervous. Then their nervousness made me even more nervous.

My mind would freeze. Instead of sounding like a competent professional looking for information from a fellow professional, I sounded like a job-seeker grasping at any opportunity. So I got one of those cheap tape recorders and began to train myself:

I learned to watch my word rate. I found that I was talking too fast because I wanted to make sure they got my message before they hung up on me. So they hung up on me. I found that the more relaxed I sounded, the more relaxed they were.

I learned to watch my volume. My best approach was to pitch my voice so that it wasn't any louder than the voice I was listening to. Otherwise, my conversation could take on the tone of an attack.

Maybe it was some kind of meditation, maybe not, but before I made the call I relaxed for a while, took deep breaths and reminded myself I was looking for an audience, not an argument.

And, though I was often tempted to do so, I never, never, never, never interrupted—even if it sounded like everything was going down the tubes.

For example, in those cases where my contact read my letter and might have been interested—but felt he or she was the wrong person to give me the information I needed:

Me: It was good of you to take the time to read my letter and respond, Mr. Contact, and I appreciate your frankness. As I explained, I'm looking for information about the criteria by which people in the aftermarket industry might seek outside sources to improve their data gathering activity. Does that idea suggest anyone else you know who might be able to give me the information I need? I would be most grateful for your help and would not use your name without your permission.

People, who would have liked to be helpful but didn't know how, often knew others who *did* know how. Sometimes they volunteered their names. Or, I had to ask. Either way, it was good manners—and good sense—to promise not to use their name without permission. Each time I got permission, it made my future contacts a great deal more effective. Using the name of someone they knew (Fred Contact suggested you would be the right person to see) improved my score.

My contact read my Communication, does not wish to get involved, and wants to dispose of me as quickly as possible.

I told myself, "OK, you can't win them all." But even this response didn't mean a dead end. It simply meant that my paragraph about my achievement had failed to generate the interest I was looking for. So, it was back to the drawing board. Perhaps a different achievement, such as training, management, trouble-shooting? By this time I had a number to choose from and there is no law against writing to someone more than once. Yes, I felt silly doing it. But I also felt angry. Why wasn't everyone decent enough to at least respond? Why doesn't everyone get a good feeling from helping other people?

Sometimes it was my fault. Instead of rehearsing for the phone call and sticking to the script, I tried a nervous ad-lib and it sounded that way. The result—a very crisp refusal to get involved with me, or a request for my resume. Both of these proved to be the same idea in different forms. What next? Another letter.

Dear-Non-Interested-Contact:

I want to apologize for sending you the attached. Obviously it was a mistaken approach, and for that I'm truly sorry. But I would like to learn where I went wrong, and only you can help me.

That's why I'm taking the liberty of contacting you once again in hopes of getting the information I'm looking for.

Why should you help someone you've never even met? Maybe you yourself received help at an important time in your life. Or, maybe you just like the feeling that comes with lending a hand. Whatever the case, my research showed you're the ideal person to give me the information I need about the criteria by which aftermarket industry might seek outside sources to improve their data gathering activity.

If I'm going in the wrong direction, you could tell me that. If I'm going to need additional skills, you could tell me that, as well. It won't take very long and would be a good thing to do.

So can we try again? I'll call on Thursday, if I may, and set a date at your convenience.

Once again, thanks for any advice you could give me.

Signed

As angry and disappointed as I was, I was careful to be as humble as possible. But I was just not going to let up, and I wanted the contact to know that. And if someone else was short-stopping my communications, I wanted them to know that, too. A PC and postage was all I needed, plus the anger to motivate my keeping this up forever, if necessary.

Part 13:
Conducting a Contact
Conversation:

One of the first things I told about myself in that church basement had to do with my lack of verbal skills, particularly when it came to talking about me. If I had a tough time with people I knew, when it came to total strangers, forget it. I've already noted that when it comes to glad-handing people I've haven't met before, I'm like the Walter Brennan character in those reruns of "Red River." There he is, doing his squint-eyed study of the approach of a still-distant figure and muttering to John Wayne about how he didn't like strangers. His reason reflected the philosophy of the rugged, go-it-alone Amurrrican: "No stranger ever good-newsed me."

What is this great fear we have of people we don't know? Old Walt resolved his uncertainties about each new face by waiting until the Duke shot him. This procedure may have relieved his tension, but it had a profoundly counter-productive effect on making contacts. Luckily, expanding his list of contacts wasn't what he was after. It was, however, what I was after.

If this contact was someone I already knew, no worry. The ice had been broken and we had the basis for the kind of small talk that got us started. But what if we were strangers to each other? What if we both felt awkward and found it difficult to set the right tone? Now here's the funny part. While actually working on a project, research was my strong suit. I could ask questions of total strangers and feel perfectly at ease because *my questions were project-oriented*. Therefore, I had the authority to ask them.

Well, this was my new project: getting positive response from people I didn't know by overcoming my own self-conscious behavior. I began practicing making conversation with strangers in everyday social situations. What I found was that I couldn't change my own personality—not at fifty. But what I could do—and did—was change my focus. Instead of making awkward attempts to overcome my own discomfort, I focused on the fact that the other party to our conversation may have been feeling equally self-conscious. So I concentrated on his/her feelings of stress rather than my own. I made it my objective to put the *other party* at ease. Like I did at the work-fairs and conventions, I practiced the natural human need to communicate by introducing myself and asking a friendly question:

Me: Hi, my name is David Abel. I'm here because I'm an old college friend of (our host/hostess). We've been out of touch for years and just bumped into each other a few weeks ago. How about you?

Nothing to it. By establishing a mutual interest, I was able to reduce the stress of getting my dialogue started. Now the conversation had a specific track on which to run. And it was easy. I discovered, however, that there was one caveat: a few of the people who were willing to see me were still a bit cynical about my stated purpose. It was as if they had made a secret bet with themselves that, all my protestations to the contrary, I was really out for a job. One contact was very direct:

They: Bottom line, what are you after? Do you really want information about the aftermarket industry, or do you want a job?"

I now admit that it caught me by surprise. A knee-jerk reaction would have been in the nature of, "Sure! The sooner the better! I've been out for weeks and it's beginning to get to me!" What saved me was my habit of slow response. Instead of answering on the echo of the question, which I couldn't have done, anyway, I stalled for a moment by offering a compliment:

Me: That's a valid question, Mr. Contact, and I can understand your asking it.

Then, not being too good at adlibbing, I fell back on what I had written:

Me: As I explained in my letter, my expertise is data management, not aftermarket. I'm not even sure by what criteria my skills would be evaluated in this environment. That's what I'm here to find out. Out of regard for your time, I'd like to ask my question, make some notes and be on my way.

Was I telling the truth, the whole truth and nothing but the truth? As I think back on that moment, I wonder. Did I say what I said to keep the Contact Conversation alive, or did I mean it? In retrospect, I believed every word of it. The pain and humiliation of being thrown out on my ear after all those years was not something I would have wanted to repeat by getting yet another JOB. As far as getting *work* in the aftermarket industry was concerned, well, I would have to know a good deal more about it, wouldn't I?

And what about the contact? Was he asking the question to psych me out, or did he have a job for me? I found this to be a possible result of every meeting. There was always the chance that, if not at the outset, then during the course of our conversation, the contact would realize that he/she might have use for some of the results I had achieved.

A more frequent and a subtler test was my contact's request to see my resume. This was easier to answer, since I did not as yet have a resume. How could I write one, when I was not sure by what criteria my skills would be evaluated in this environment? That's what I was there to find out.

Me: I plan to write my resume based on what I learn from you today. As I explained in my letter, my expertise is data management, not aftermarket. I'm not even sure by what criteria my skills would be evaluated in this environment. That's what I'm here to find out. Out of regard for your time, I'd like to ask my question, make some notes and be on my way.

I must admit that learning to recite what I had written was beginning to get to me. I felt like some kind of a trained monkey, even though I was doing the training. The church group picked it up, too, and began picking on me. "Hypocrite" was the kindest term they used. "You're trying to be somebody else," they accused, "It doesn't even sound like you."

At first, I thought they were right. All of this *was* phony. But then the facilitator came to my rescue. She started with a reminder that we weren't there to criticize one another. Then she went on to point out that the new people I was meeting had no idea of what I had sounded like in the past. To them, I was the only David Abel they knew, and if they were favorably impressed by what they heard, that was all that mattered. "The fact is," she said, "you sounded more confident and more convincing than the day you started."

I realized she was right. By reaching into my paragraphs, I was not only being truthful, but consistent. And, most important, I was spared the need to adlib on the spur of a vital moment. In my experience, the impression I made during those first few seconds was what caused my contact to decide whether or not to help me achieve the objectives of a Contact Conversation by:

1. Telling me the criteria by which people in that particular specialty would evaluate the kind of results I could achieve, so that I could create a resume that would be right on target.

2. Possibly referring me to other people in the industry so that I could expand my knowledge of the business, as well as improve my potential of getting work from different sources by expanding my network of contacts.

3. Telling me how and where to get the additional information or even training I might need in order to better satisfy certain criteria.

Part 14:
Asking the one question I had promised to ask.

Me:	Thank you for taking the time to see me, Ms./Mr. Contact. As I explained in my letter, the after-market industry may have a particular need for the kind of results I can achieve—like the branch-reporting program that helped to improve productivity by 25%. But to make sure, I wanted to talk to people like you who really know the industry from the inside. Out of regard for your time, I wanted to ask just one question, make some notes and be on my way. Is that all right?

I can't stress often enough how big a departure it was for me to talk about *"the kind of results I can achieve."* But I had no choice. How else was I to present myself as someone worth talking to? Not with the story of my working life, but with the one achievement that persuaded the contact to meet with me.

They:	I've been wondering about that. What's the one question you wanted to ask?
Me:	By what criteria would the aftermarket industry seek outside sources to get the kind of results I've described?
They:	That's a good question. Let me think about that.
Me:	Is it all right if I take some notes?

I worked on that question for a long time. What I had hoped to establish (and did, more often than not) was a mutual interest that would make the Contact Conversation work. So I kept it short and to the point. I avoided the word, 'you.' My gut feeling was that if I asked, "would *you* seek," I would be over-personalizing the question and implying that, instead of information about how to find work, I was looking for work from *him*. On more than one occasion, the response began with some comment like, "Well. I can't speak for the industry, but I can give you my own opinion." Needless to say, that was OK with me.

I soon came to realize that this was the very first time my contacts had been asked that question. What gave me that impression was the frequency with which they commented on the question itself before they offered an answer. "That's a good question" or "That's an interesting question," or "That's a provocative question" was either a compliment or a stall to give them time to think about it. Either way, I was ready to help.

Part 15:
The skill of taking good notes:

Those instances where my Contact Conversation really worked out in accordance with my wildest dreams, I found myself getting a lot of vital information. And some, not so vital. And some so far off the track that it wasn't really information at all. But the problem was that there was no way to tell in advance what I would have to remember and what was instantly forgettable. Without competent notes, this would prove to be awkward.

Then I turned the desk around and looked at the situation from the contact's point of view. He/she was giving time and energy to give me what I had said I wanted—an insider's view of the criteria by which the aftermarket industry might seek outside sources to get the kind of results I've described. Just how detailed did I want that information to be? Plenty! But if I was just sitting there and just making great eye contact, what would be the point of loading me up with a lot of data I probably wouldn't remember? Why not give me a few brief answers and then see me out the door?

Unless I knew how to take good notes.

Who doesn't know how to take good notes? In my experience, most people. Not that everyone can't listen and write. Anybody who's been to school is accustomed to doing that. But I would sneak a look around that table in the church basement and see that the various styles of doodles were the same as those I saw at group meetings where I used to work. I remember feeling superior because my note-taking was so exact. As silly as it seemed at the time, I put it near the top of my list of skills. And that was before I ever had to focus on note-taking as a competitive element in getting work. Mind you, those doodlers might focus on improving a tennis stroke as if they were on the way to the Open. But note-taking? Who had to think twice about it?

I did. I had to decide what kind of note-taking materials would make the best impression on my contact. Those little memo pads fit easily inside my jacket pocket and they worked fine during job-fairs and conventions. But that was to note names and addresses, and here I was after a lot more. I thought that the way I took notes would send a lot of signals to my contact. That's why I decided that, to make the most professional impression, it would make sense to use the tools the professionals use—a yellow, legal-size pad and a black, felt-tipped pen. They worked great when I was doing research because they commanded instant recognition.

Sure, because of that legal size, I needed a special folder. But the time I took opening it, taking out my pad and getting ready, gave my contact time to think about his/her answer to my question. To provide even more time, I drew a line down the middle of the first page and block-printed the word CRITERIA at the head of the left-hand column. I was careful to print it big enough so that my contact could read it.

CRITERIA	

That first time I was filled with a certain anxiety. Or, to make it plainer, I was scared to death. Sure, I had done my share of project research, but a lot of that had to do with technical information or wordy opinions that I was free to reduce to their essentials. But in this situation, if the information I was about to receive had any importance whatever—and the criteria by which that industry might go outside to give me work certainly rates pretty high—I sensed that I would need that information in some detail. I would also need it in order of importance.

There was always the possibility that some of the information would have to be expanded or further explained. That's what the right-hand column was for. I felt that once I had demonstrated that I was serious about exploring the aftermarket industry and was not just letting the information go in one ear and out the other, I would learn a lot more. And I did.

Maybe I left out that, among my other liabilities, I write like a ransom note. Over the years, to make sure I could later read what I wrote, I learned to block print. Not big, just regular size. But now I wanted what I was writing—excuse me, printing—to be seen at a distance. Everything went more smoothly when my contacts knew they were being noted and quoted correctly. So I went back to learning how to block print BIG. It took a bit more time, but it gave my contact more time to think. The felt-tipped pen is not only a slick mover and makes a thicker line, but black is a highly visible color.

Since I had to concentrate on listening and noting, my lack of verbal skills never came up. All I had to say was enough to keep the contact talking. Having spent a good deal of my working life among people who thought that listening was simply the time needed to inhale before speaking, I wouldn't have interrupted even if I knew how. But there was always the temptation, upon hearing a friendly criterion, to break in with the story of my life. I didn't. Nor did I betray (at least I *think* I didn't) that I had heard some of the criteria before.

That's the one caveat to this approach. While the terminology might be different, many of the criteria are essentially the same. Whether I was meeting with Fred Friendly, or Charlie Smith or any of the contacts my communications generated, once we got down to cases there were a number of parallels. I found that the specific words each Contact used were important to me because they were important to them. So while this is a report of a typical discussion, the language is specific to this one example:

They:	Well, first thing would be the tools. It's not the most important—maybe the last—but it's the common denominator for MIS. According to what you wrote, you're used to working with spreadsheets, functional web page design, EXCEL, etc. That's all to the good.
Me:	(Repeating as I BLOCK PRINTED) THE TOOLS. OK, I've made a note of that. What else?
They:	Every outfit has a different system—or think they do. I would say another key criterion—what everyone wants, inside or out, is someone who is a quick study. For

example, you'd have to learn their operations management and how they planned to use the data.

Me: Let me add that, then. A QUICK STUDY…HOW OPERATIONS MGT USES DATA. I've got that. What else is there?

They: Whatever systems you develop had better be robust enough to run failure-free without tweaking. That only aggravates the top floor.

Me: ROBUST SYSTEMS—TO RUN FAILURE FREE WITHOUT TWEAKING AND MGT. AGGRAVATION. I've added that. What else?

They: The aftermarket business survives on fast, accurate, data transfer, analysis and reporting. If you know how to design a report that answers questions instead of provoking them, you should do OK.

Me: KNOW-HOW TO DESIGN REPORTS THAT ANSWER QUESTIONS VS. PROVOKING THEM. Great! I've got that. What's next?

They: Frankly, unless we're overloaded or are in a crush situation, we ourselves don't go outside that much. That's because this kind of work calls for a lot of interface with inside people in other departments. An outsider would have to be a damn good communicator.

Me: A DAMN GOOD COMMUNICATOR—MUST INTERFACE WITH INSIDE PEOPLE IN OTHER DEPARTMENTS.

They: (laughs) If there is going to be some kind of permanent record of this, I'd rather you didn't quote me that way.

Me: No problem. I'll just change that to VERY. Is that OK? What's next?

They: The bottom line, I guess. Time and money.

Me: TIME AND MONEY. How do you mean that?

They: Nobody takes on extra people unless they've got an emergency—a really bad problem with a really close deadline. But nobody budgets for emergencies. So the extra cost becomes a major factor. It's not only the time, it's the money.

Me: Thank you for your time and the information you've given me. May I take just another moment to review what I've learned?

They: Sure, go ahead.

Me: (Reading from my pad.)

CRITERIA	
THE TOOLS	EXCEL, SPREAD -
	SHEETS, WEB PAGE
	DESIGN, ETC
A QUICK STUDY	HOW OPS MGT
	USES DATA
ABILITY TO PUT	RUN FAILURE-FREE
TOGETHER A	WITHOUT TWEAKING
ROBUST SYSTEM	& Mgt AGGRAVATION
KNOW-HOW TO	ANSWER QUESTIONS
DESIGN REPORTS	VS.PROVOKING THEM
VERY	
A ~~DAMN~~ GOOD	MUST INTERFACE
COMMUNICATOR	WITH INSIDE PEOPLE
	IN OTHER
	DEPARTMENTS
TIME AND MONEY	NO BUDGETS FOR
	EMERGENCIES

The real fear I felt about asking my question disappeared with the first answer and never came back. From that first answer on, I understood the power of appealing to someone's expertise and paying them the respect of recording what they had to say. Actually, I was doing more than putting my contacts on record. My question and note-taking offered a number of other advantages:

1. If my contact was in any way curious about how we had gotten to be on a first-name basis, my question and my note pad moved the focus of the conversation elsewhere. I began to think of it as my '3-G' opening: Greeting, Gratitude and Getting down to the business at hand. It took but a moment to say hello, express my thanks for the opportunity, and refer to my letter:

Me: As I explained in my letter, I'm here to learn by what criteria the (aftermarket industry) would seek outside sources to get the kind of results I've described.

2. Actually, nobody timed me. I had asked for 15 minutes, but once they started thinking—really thinking—about those criteria, they would go into some detail. Not all of it was worth noting, but I got an insider's view of a particular business or industry I could not have gotten any other way.

3. I got the truth. At least I'm pretty sure I did. When people speak 'for the record' even though it's to someone of no authority, like me, they get careful. That bit about retracting the word 'damn' also applied in those cases where we got on the topic of the kind of results they were looking for. Instead of some impossible, over-the-top number, I got the straight story.

4. If they were ready to take the time to review my notes, maybe they would also take the time to consider additional criteria. This was particularly important when the contact left out some criterion that would make me look especially good. For example, I could do a lot more than design and implement systems. I could manage a project team. I could take a program into the field and train people in its use. I could write the administrative and incentive programs it might take to achieve total success. But would any of these be important enough to include in the way I presented my skills? I would have to ask.

Me: How about the ability to manage a project team?

They: Oh, sure. That goes without saying. Unless it's the kind of project you can complete by yourself, you're going to have to be a strong team manager. Stronger yet when you're an outsider and the team is inside. That's part of what I meant when I said you had to be a good communicator.

Me: Then let me add that to the list, OK? STRONG TEAM MANAGER. Then how about being able to take a program into the field and train people in its use? Is that important?

They: Well, speaking for us, we have our own trainers. So that would be of little interest. But there is no training department that I know of at Acme Parts, for example, so they might need more in-depth support.

Me: I'll make a note about that and get in touch.

With the addition I had encouraged, my list now told a more complete story.

CRITERIA	
THE TOOLS	EXCEL, SPREAD -
	SHEETS, WEB PAGE
	DESIGN, ETC
A QUICK STUDY	HOW OPS MGT
	USES DATA
ABILITY TO PUT	RUN FAILURE-FREE
TOGETHER A	WITHOUT TWEAKING
ROBUST SYSTEM	& Mgt AGGRAVATION
KNOW-HOW TO	ANSWER QUESTIONS
DESIGN REPORTS	VS.PROVOKING THEM
VERY	
A ~~DAMN~~ GOOD	MUST INTERFACE
COMMUNICATOR	WITH INSIDE PEOPLE
	IN OTHER
	DEPARTMENTS
TIME AND MONEY	NO BUDGETS FOR
	EMERGENCIES
STRONG TEAM	YOU'RE AN OUTSIDER
MANAGER	AND THE TEAM'S
	INSIDE
ABILITY TO TRAIN	NOT HERE - BUT AT
THE TRAINERS	ACME PARTS?

It was easy to tell when the contact was enjoying the role of the mentor. There I was, a 'student' eager to learn—so eager that I was taking careful notes. For all I knew, my contact may have even been making a comparison between my respectful behavior and that of members of his/her regular staff. Whatever the case, I would begin to hear verbal cues whenever the contact referred to some situation within his or her own organization. I found myself 'pronoun sensitive.' Phrases like 'speaking for us' or 'we ourselves' moved the discussion from a general view of the industry to the practices of that particular company. There might have been a number of reasons why my contact was talking this way:

1. A meeting of The Association of Managers of Over-Staffed Departments could take place in a phone booth. I knew from my own past experience that 'lean and mean' is a cute slogan, but it put one hell of a strain on the people who had to do the actual work. Which is why it was a rare department head who wasn't after his/her management to budget more help. And the plea was so often the same: "I need somebody who can…" The answer was always the same: "Send me a memo and I'll think it over." The memo was always the same—a list of job criteria. Small wonder, then, that his or her own needs and practices were up front in the mind of every assertive manager I contacted.

2. Any professional needs to stay alert to what's happening in the industry. One good reason is that during a period of professional musical chairs one never knows which will be the next to be pulled. Another is that it pays to keep competitive to whatever is going on. This calls for a constant evaluation of what the contact's own organization is doing vs. the competition.

3. There was always the wonderful possibility that my contacts didn't know they could get my particular combination of skills and experience on a rental basis—or that their organization could get the kind of results I had achieved. When they started to tell me about how they operate, were they suggesting that *we* could get together? I had to find out.

So I had to learn when it was safe for me to take a shot—and I mean that, literally—because that's what the first letters of each step I took spelled out: S-H-O-T.

Select a criterion: I didn't have to rely on my nonexistent ability to adlib because I now had a whole list. I just started from the top. Simple, right?

Highlight some experience that met the criterion. Once again, I didn't have to make it up. I just borrowed from my paragraph.

Offer some kind of evidence to prove I could do what they wanted done. All the samples I had taken from my office were still in my briefcase, so I just pulled them out.

Test how I was doing with some question—just to make sure we were on the same page.

When the first chance came, I wasn't that well prepared. I felt that I was taking too much time and I was overstaying my welcome. That made me feel awkward, which made me sound anxious rather than confident. I wasn't going to let that happen again. By the next time, I had worked out a way of introducing the idea.

Me: You've given me quite a list, Ms./Mr. Contact. May I take another moment or two just to make sure I understand your thinking? For example, you emphasized the importance of being a *quick study.*

In the project I referred to in my letter, where I assumed the responsibility for getting more timely and accurate performance reports, *a quick overview I conducted tracked the distribution of each element of the data* to determine who was using it and why.

Here's the research form I e-mailed to each branch manager that enabled me to simplify reporting by dropping unused or unusable data. These findings helped me to persuade management that a sharper focus on the most vital data would reduce the time-and-error factor. *How does this compare with what you had in mind when you said, "Quick Study?"*

That test question was the biggy. It meant that after 45 seconds of talking about myself I had to shut up and give my contact a chance to respond. This was no 'yes' or 'no' answer, either. "How does this compare…" is a request for information…for an opinion…perhaps, even, for some kind of commitment. So I just held my breath and listened for the answer.

Can I stop here for just a moment and admit that my earliest interviews were nothing like this? They were more of the traditional, I-speak-someone-listens variety. Since I was flying blind it was only natural that I'd buzz off in all directions, repeating myself, falling all over myself and trying to guess what my listener was thinking. If I stopped talking, I would get a look that seemed to ask, "Finished?" This would be followed by a look that said, "Thanks for coming by." Sometimes, the look would be accompanied by a grunt, but that's the closest I came to any verbal response. It was to avoid that stare and grunt that I designed each test question with words like 'how' or 'what.' They require an answer.

OK, what's a good answer? Easy—any form of positive response. Something as simple as, "That's the kind of thing I had in mind" confirmed the accuracy of my understanding and was my invitation to continue. It was even better when I was asked some question about how I had handled some specific detail: "How exactly did you conduct the research?" This request for more details indicated a real interest on the part of the contact in how I had done what I had done.

Me:	What I have next is *a thorough understanding of how data applies to operations management.*
	As a result of my research, *I was able to eliminate almost 20% of the present entries,* without any significant "blind spots."
	Here's a before-and-after exhibit I designed as a handout for my presentation to management.
	What's your opinion of my understanding of how data applies to operations management?

It had never occurred to me to save a lot of the material I had developed during my years on the job. Once I found out how interested some of my contacts were, I finally cleaned out my desk at home and resurrected a lot of reports, presentations and even some memos that would help to prove my skills. Those I no longer had, I recreated.

Me:	Your interest in the *ability to design robust system*s appeals to me.
	I have only one standard for system design—it has to *function failure-free without tweaking.*
	Here's a typical downtime chart I used to keep for every system I either designed myself or had directed the design. As you can see by the notes, what little downtime there was came about due to management add-ons to the existing system.
	How do these figures compare with your own standards for system performance?

Asking what's going on in my contact's business would have been considered kind of nervy if I hadn't laid the groundwork for this conversation. But I was trying to interest my contacts in renting the kind of results I could produce. These results had to be an improvement—otherwise, why should they be interested?

Me: Which brings us to *experienced in strong team management.*

I had to assemble and direct a diverse team from a number of different departments each with its own agenda. None of us had ever worked together, but the results were still expected to be on budget and on time. So *I established a weekly 'status meeting,'* with published *reports that gave name credit* for every bit of progress. At the first meeting I distributed *special mugs,* half of which read 'on budget' and the other half 'on time.' Using that theme, my assignments and direction went down as easily as the coffee or tea.

Here's the set of mugs. For another team situation, I used a t-shirt. Corny, perhaps, but very effective in getting results—and a great way for an outsider to break the ice.

How well do you think this meets your criterion of strong team management?

By personalizing my test question I was walking on eggs just a little bit. But I took courage from the fact that my earlier answers were all positive. These positive reactions meant that I was meeting the criteria. Was there a job there? Was there work there? To find out, I felt I had to break the barrier between me on the outside and them on the inside.

Me: You also said I would need the *know-how to design reports that answer questions rather than provoke them.* I think I know just what you meant, but allow me a moment to verify it.

As I explained in my letter, *the reporting system I set up used an Excel spreadsheet template to facilitate entering complete and accurate data.* A Visual Basic application we wrote checked them for accuracy. A web page created for corporate management offered an assortment of reports, accepted report requests, translated these into SQL commands, transmitted them to the Central MIS server for execution and presented the results.

Here are some figures showing comparative results. The fact that the data was so timely and useful improved the compliance rate among regional managers from 71% to near 100%.

How does this compare with the kind of report design you had in mind?

Each of these **SHOT**s had one thing in common: I had to do very little 'lecturing.' For me, that was the whole idea. What I wanted was a discussion—and that's a two-way street. I had enough of those tell-me-about-yourself monologues to last me forever. As I have often said, I'm lousy at them, anyway. Also, for every positive response I got, my self-approval rating went up. Here was confirmation that I had marketable skills. I found my ego coming back.

Part 16:
The return of the ego.

Maybe it was part of my denial. Better yet, no 'maybe's' about it, it *was* part of my denial that the way I got dumped had that much of an effect on my feeling of self-worth. Speaking personally, I never gave much credit to the idea that people—men in particular—get their identity and a sense of their own worth through their work. In the past, I'd read one of those no-work-no-self-worth kind of articles and just snort and turn to the ball scores. Now I know different—at least where I'm concerned.

Now, I had worked with all levels of ego. I had worked with people whose egos were so huge they seemed to enter a room before their owners, and put up posters telling how great they were. And I felt that I held my own. But the impact of the afternoon I got fired stayed with me. I found myself replaying that scene with different kinds of dialogue—seeing myself in a range of roles from Nathan Hale at the noose to Sidney Carton at the guillotine. But no matter how many brave lines I came up with, the sad fact was that I was thinking like a victim.

When you think like a victim—or at least when *I* think like a victim—I tend to start seeing the reasoning behind my victimhood, rather than the unfairness of it. Let's see if I can make that any clearer. *I begin to see the justification of the other side.* My first thought was that this was my social worker background taking over. But, in reality, I finally had to face the fact that what had happened had convinced me that I wasn't as good as I thought I was. I was subscribing to management's belief that I was totally dispensable. There were, I imagined, a number of people in that room when my name came up. They must have looked at each other and wondered, however briefly, if my absence from now on would make that much of a difference. The consensus was, quite obviously, that it would not.

Now then, if they felt that way, why shouldn't everyone feel that way? Why shouldn't every contact I made share the opinion that I had so little to offer? And I wasn't alone in this belief. I lost count of the number of times someone in my group actually declared their own worthlessness by making statements like:

"Everyone says you need an MBA and I don't have an MBA."

"There aren't any jobs open for (fill it in.)"
"I couldn't live on what they were willing to pay."

The rest of us, on hearing these declarations, sounded like a bunch of chickens clucking our sympathy. And talk about victims—chickens either had their eggs stolen or wound up on a platter. And I was one of them. Which is why, when my fellow 'inmates' were talking that way, I never questioned what I was hearing. It was only after my early Contact Conversations that I might have asked them:

Me: Just who is this 'everyone' who says you need an MBA? Is it really *everyone* or was it just one interview? Was that the only criterion? And weren't you doing this work for years without an MBA?

If there 'aren't any jobs open' does that mean nobody ever leaves town, retires, dies or simply quits? And did you find this out by asking, "Hey, are there any jobs open?" and being told there weren't? Maybe there's a better way of finding out.

As to compensation, how much would you pay me, right here and now, for this great life preserver? Well here, on dry land, not very much. But what if you were drowning? What if you could be convinced that you badly needed what I had to sell? Would that alter your idea of what that something was worth? Take another look at how you've been communicating your own value.

Of course, my great analysis of those statements came after the fact. And the fact is that I *do* have valuable and marketable skills. How do I know? First, there were those paragraphs—each an achievement that produced the results management was after. Second, there were people who were willing to meet with me on the strength of those paragraphs and give me the guidance I needed. Third, my contacts gave me lists of criteria and I could meet most if not all of them.

So why did it take me as long as it did to finally get the work I was after? I made a simple, stupid mistake, that's why.

Part 17:
Listening under pressure.

In my opinion, it was the adrenaline. Under the stress of meeting with the contact, something started pumping the extra energy we needed to deal with what was happening. Could this have affected someone's hearing? It sure did mine. I was so busy trying to figure ways in which I could 'sell myself—something I could never have done in a million years—that I must have missed a lot that went on. Even though I came from a profession where listening was the big thing, back then, I was listening *as* the authority. That's quite different from listening *to* the authority. I had to retrain myself to be a good listener.

To a good listener, precisely what is being said, the order in which it is said, and the implication of what is being said is all-important. Even though I had made careful notes, I felt there were instances when I had to verify my understanding of what I was being told. Sure enough, there were times when my interpretation of some criterion was close, but not right on the money. The first time that happened I thought, "Uh-oh, this is going downhill in a hurry." But as it turned out, my contact's willingness to set me straight had a lot going for it—as long as I knew how to listen:

They: That's very good, but it's not quite what I had in mind when I said 'quick study.' What I'm on the lookout for is the kind of thinking that can assess the problem just by looking at the results we're getting—without waiting for input from anyone—including me.

The temptation to interrupt and correct the situation was so strong, and I was so focused on what I could hardly wait to say, that I wasn't listening as carefully as I should have. Otherwise, I would have been alert to the full implication of what was being said:

What I'm on the lookout for!

Perhaps not the best grammar I ever heard, but the best kind of response. My contact is looking and so am I. But how actively is he/she looking? Are we talking about some long-range plan or is there something more immediate under consideration? In plain English, have I stumbled on an opening that has not yet been posted? Or, has meeting me and sharing in this discussion given the contact some ideas about improving departmental productivity?

But I registered none of the above. I mean I went right by it. Talk about stupid. The only way I could possibly explain the lapse was that I wasn't expecting it, so I didn't really hear it. I thought the way I regrouped and responded was good, though.

Me:	Let me clarify how I functioned in the case I've just described. What I started with was just this—*a management directive outlining what they wanted improved.* I took it from there and immediately went into system design. I felt that asking for input *with this survey*, while I was already working on these improvements would give everyone a chance to have their say. *It turned out to be good policy—and good politics. How does that measure up to the kind of thinking you're on the lookout for?*

I then corrected my earlier mistake. Upon hearing that I now had everything right and that my contact and I were on the same page, it was time to say 'thank you' and that 'you've been a big help,' both of which were true. But that wonderful phrase was now clearly in my mind: *what I'm on the lookout for.*

Once my listening became focused, those positive phrases never escaped me again. Anything that suggested the contact wasn't entirely satisfied by the status quo was my signal to ask the '*Is there anything else…*' question:

We're always trying to improve our percentage of accuracy.

Our productivity could always be better.

It's hard to find people who can…

If I had responded to any of these comments with, "Hey, then, how about me? I'm your guy!" I'm not to sure what would have happened. There were just too many risks. First, there was the risk to my credibility. After sending this contact a number of communications assuring him that I wouldn't jump him for a job, there I'd be, doing just that.

Next was the risk of giving the impression that he couldn't speak frankly to me without my taking immediate advantage of it. If our relationship was to last past this meeting (and I certainly hoped that it would) this was a time to help it develop.

The biggest risk of all would have been failing to deal with any doubts he still may have had in his mind. That's where the question came from:

Me: From what you've learned about me, what else would you need to know in order to be sure I had the kind of skills you're on the lookout for?

In my opinion, the question didn't squeeze too hard. There was no timing built into it, no 'how soon will you be making up your mind?' This was all to the good as far as I was concerned. It meant there had been no opening posted. I was not only first in line; I was the only one in line. And he confirmed all my concerns. He told me he would need some kind of resume he could use to convince other authorities to budget the position. Good! He was soon going to see the most accurate resume he had ever come across—because he had just helped me to write it. But there was one thing more:

Me: In the meantime, is there anyone else you would suggest that I talk to? According to my notes you suggested Acme Parts.

No matter how positive this meeting sounded, I knew better than to let the opportunity to make yet another contact go by—particularly one with a personal introduction. I felt that my request let this contact off the hook, so to speak. He'd been generous enough to make the recommendation in the first place. By letting him know I planned to follow up, I was also letting him know that in case what he had in mind didn't work out—or didn't work out immediately—he had opened another door for me. Besides, if he decided to rent rather than buy my skills, I would need as many renters as I could handle. I found that a lot of people knew their opposite numbers at other companies (some may have worked together at one time) and would be willing to give me the names. When they were, the first three words of my Contact Communication to them were all set: "Personal regards from—."

Part 18:
The 'resume' my contact helped me to write.

Recalling my contact's request for ASAP, since a resume is a summary, I wrote out a summary of our conversation.

Summary of the conversation with (name of contact) on (date)

Purpose of our conversation: To review the criteria by which (the aftermarket industry) would seek outside sources to achieve results: such as improving the accuracy level of reported data by more than half, with a compliance rate improvement from 71% to near 100%. For example, On one recent project, I assumed the responsibility for getting more timely and accurate performance reports from 24 regional management teams that were already "too busy," and to make these accessible to corporate management personnel located in 6 headquarters worldwide

The criteria you provided, and how I met them:

Quick study: What I started with was a management directive outlining what they wanted improved. I took it from there and immediately went into system design. I also asked for input, to give everyone who wanted a voice in whatever changes I would introduce a chance to have a say. As a result, I was able to review each element of the data to determine who was using it and why; enabling me to simplify reporting. To persuade management to sign off, my presentation showed that a sharper focus on the most vital data would reduce our time-and-error factor.

Thorough understanding of how data applies to operations management: As a result, I was able to eliminate almost 20% of the present entries, without any significant "blind spots."

Ability to design robust systems: This enabled me to direct the design team toward a system that would function failure-free without tweaking.

Experienced in strong team management: I had to assemble and direct a diverse team from a number of different departments, each with its own agenda. None of us had ever worked together, but the results were still expected to be on budget and on time. So I established a weekly 'status meeting,' with published reports that gave name credit for every bit of progress. At the first meeting, I distributed special mugs, half of which read 'on budget' and the other half 'on time.' Using that theme, my assignments and direction went down as easily as the coffee or tea.

Know-how to design reports that answer questions rather than provoke them: I led the team in the design and implementation of secure and restricted pages on the corporate website. The web page created for regional managers prompted for and accepted submissions of regional reports using an Excel spreadsheet template to facilitate entering complete and accurate data. The spreadsheets were emailed to Central MIS where a Visual Basic application we wrote checked them for accuracy, integrated those passing the tests into a SQL Server database, and returned by e-mail acknowledgments to the senders requesting corrections if necessary.

The web page created for corporate management offered an assortment of reports, accepted report requests, translated these into SQL commands, transmitted them to the Central MIS server for execution, and presented the results. We created the web pages using a combination of Microsoft Frontpage, Active Server Pages, and VB Script.

The fact that the data was so timely and useful improved the compliance rate among regional managers from 71% to near 100%.

Experienced in meeting time and budget requirements: Both were right on the money.

Skilled in tools: Power user of Microsoft office applications (especially Word, Excel, Frontpage) expert with Active Server Pages, SQL, VB Script to name just the headliners

David M. Abel   Telephone:

Address   FAX

City State Zip   Email

There's no one more boring in the whole world than a recent convert to anything. If I had a nickel for every account I've listened to about a new, wonderful, health routine a friend had just discovered, I wouldn't have to work. Which is why, I guess, the people in the church basement got those funny looks on their faces when I finally decided to 'share' my experience with the Contact Conversations I had been having. I made the mistake common to all converts and got carried away.

What did it, I guess, was the wonderful feeling I got from finally having a conversation that wasn't just polite talk. God knows I'd had my share of those, followed by the sad fact that it had led to nothing but another rejection. There, in my hand, was my yellow pad with my notes that showed there was a need for the skills I had for sale or rent. What better encouragement could I have gotten? Here was proof that I was still of value. Here was proof that I was on the right track. I even passed my summary of the conversation around.

Did I get a round of applause? Not hardly. I got a split vote. A few thought it sounded like a good approach. The majority competed with each other to come up with reasons why what had just worked so well wouldn't work:

Because people have learned to see through that 'information' bit.
Because people have no time to get involved in my problems.
Because everyone wants to see a resume and nothing else.

I was beginning to go on the defensive when our facilitator came to my rescue. She printed two words on the blackboard: "BECAUSE" and "UNLESS." The gist of her explanation was that these two words summed up the difference between a pessimist and a realist. A pessimist, when presented with a new idea—or at least one differing from what he believed to be true—would immediately tell you why it wouldn't work BECAUSE. And whatever the BECAUSE was would become a self-fulfilling prophecy. Failure was bound to result for the reason specified.

A realist, on the other hand, also believes the idea won't work, but feels that it can be fixed so that it *will* work. The key word the realist uses is UNLESS, as in:

It won't work for me unless I can persuade people that I'm worth talking to.

True enough—for me, as well. That's why I expended the time and effort to create the best paragraphs I could. If nothing else, I wanted to give the impression that I was no lightweight, but someone who would be interesting to talk to. When my contact referred to my communication—maybe even by quoting from it—I took that as a compliment.

It won't work for me unless I can persuade people to respond to my request for information.

I tried a number of different questions until I found the one that got me the best response. By what criteria would the (aftermarket industry) seek outside sources to get the kind of results I've described? If the contact said, outright, "We use outside sources from time to time," all I did was make the question more direct:

Me: By what criteria would *you* seek outside sources to get the kind of results I've described?

This discussion started a major firefight. If a contact said there was work available, maybe there was a *job* available. What my fellow participants had been struggling to find were JOBS…with all the accompanying titles, benefits and a regular paycheck.

OK, fine. If there *was* a job available, maybe that would come up in the conversation. But the reason we're all here is that, up to this minute, there have been no jobs available. If I had gone job-seeking, my contacts might have refused to meet with me. That's where the whole idea of renting my skills rather than trying to sell them on a full-time basis came from. Without knowing I was being prophetic, I insisted that, given the choice between a job and a meaty project, I would be tempted to take the latter. Not that I was better off financially than any of them, but because I no longer had faith in the idea of job security.

The experience of everyone in that room was proof that everything is temporary: the non-profit jobs ran out of funding; the tech jobs were lost to newer systems; the hands-on work was lost to labor-saving devices. And when those people stopped buying because they were out of work, anyone who was selling or marketing was in trouble. Small wonder that, rather than getting involved in the costs of hiring and severance, employers are thinking part-time and projects. All I was doing was going with the flow. My idea was that doing work for three companies instead of just one made for better odds.

If I thought *that* was rough going, I was in for more. When everyone had had a chance to see my Summary of a Conversation, what I had thought had been a major difference of opinion turned out to be a pretty calm preamble. It's as if they had all rehearsed it:

"What kind of resume is this?"

Who's to say what a resume should look like? Who set the rules? I go back far enough to remember a time when not everyone had access to, let alone owned, a PC. Back then, the buckshot approach made sense: put down everything you can think of because getting it produced wasn't easy. How is it, I wonder, in this age of specialized tasking, that this habit still persists? Today, a job-seeker can detail specific experience to meet specific job criteria. But there's the rub. How many of my fellow participants in that basement, frustrated and discouraged by failed interviews, knew exactly by what criteria the successful applicant would get the job? In this case, I knew. My odd-looking resume was a summary of what I had been told my contact wanted.

The word itself means 'to summarize.' But to summarize what? My entire working life—including my summer jobs, my stint as a social worker in a high-crime area, my military experience? What does that past experience have to do with what I'm looking for today? Even more to the point, what does it have to do with what my contacts are looking for today? What I learned from my Contact Conversations was that to be effective, a resume should be a summation of *that specific conversation*—no more, no less. The individual example might differ, depending on which of my skills I wanted to feature, but the criteria would have to come from the contact. How else would I know what skills to stress?

I could guess. That's what I did when I wrote my first resumes. That's what we all did. Those resumes brought us nothing but a pretty hefty depression and a seat in the church basement.

I tried to explain this to the group—to no avail. Maybe I got started on the wrong foot by declaring that a 'dump mailing' of hundreds of resumes is a waste of time, money and, perhaps, good contacts. The fact that I had tried the same approach and failed just as they had didn't make my pronouncement any easier to accept. But it made sense: *the best source for what you put in your resume is what a potential employer said he/she would want.* True, this means you'd have to first find out what was wanted, but that's the name of the game.

I explained that I wasn't discounting the idea of responding to ads or postings. But why do only one thing? Why use only one approach? Try every avenue of contact. For example, a good ad or posting is one that provides a detailed list of the criteria. Of course the odds are that the better the ad the greater the response, and the greater the response the greater the competition. But the odds also are that most applicants will send their standard 'everything-that-sounds-good' resume and attempt to make it more specific with a covering letter. I know, because I received plenty of them when my ex-firm was looking for people. And I know what happened. Whoever was stuck with the screening job ignored the letter and matched the resume against the criteria listed in the ad. Then they put a number at the top of the resume coinciding with the number of criteria the applicant could meet. The resumes with the highest numbers would make it to the short list. The moral: if you've sent a by-guess-and-by-gosh-resume, don't wait by the phone.

I thought I was through sharing and wanted to take my seat, but the questions started coming thick and fast.

Q:	(From someone who wasn't really getting it) How could you call this a resume?
A:	Because that's what it is. A resume is a summary, and this is a summary of a conversation I had with one of my contacts.
Q:	We've already talked about the fact that resumes are sent to HR and don't get through to the decision-maker. How is this any different?
A:	This communication met all the criteria for getting through to my contact. It's as personal as can be, since I'm quoting the contact him/herself. I'm counting on the fact that an authority being quoted would want to read how well and accurately he/she was perceived. In affect, it's a resume, but it doesn't look at all like a resume. To make sure the guardians get the message, my covering letter (also personal) refers to it as a *summary*, while asking for comment and critique rather than a JOB. This gives my communication a better-than-even chance of getting read.
Q:	What about times and dates of your experience?
A:	What about them? What is to be gained by stamping a date on this information as if it had to be consumed before it got stale? This is just one case study of my skills, abilities and knowledge. Each point meets the criteria in the very language of the person who will decide whether or not they have any work for me. Besides, why create one of those chronological jobs where the reader could do the math and decide I was too old?

Q: But what about previous job titles and responsibilities?

A: Isn't it true that the most recent title means the most? So what is the point of listing a number of old titles and job responsibilities? Isn't it also true that most job responsibilities are expressed in vague, general terms rather than as specific achievements? This makes the average resume very repetitive—and therefore pretty boring.

Q: What if there were other skills worth mentioning?

A: Worth it to whom? Once I got his/her list of criteria, I tested the value of other skills I could have included. In this case, my 'how about' question resulted in an addition that came through loud and clear: STRONG TEAM MANAGER. So I included it. Why include information that *wasn't* asked for? A good rule of thumb is: that which doesn't help, can hurt.

Q: What's a 'how about' question?

A: Didn't I explain that? When you've made a list of all the criteria, you might find that your contact has left out a few that make you look very good. So, you want them in there. That's why I used the "How about the ability to…" question to get the approval to add them. The more I can add to my summary, the better I look and the more I'm worth.

Q: Does this mean that a summary that shows how you meet all the criteria will get you the job?

A: Did I fail to make clear that there *was no job*—at least no job that I knew of? If it turned out there was one, well that would have been great! But I didn't count on it. What I wanted was a conversation with someone who knew by what criteria their industry or company might go outside for the kind of results I could help to achieve.

Q: But what if they told you they never went outside?

A: That's happened. The first time that happened, I must admit I almost blew it by apologizing for taking up the time and leaving. But, before I could, my contact continued with: "But if we ever *did* decide to go outside…" and we were off and running. After all, my letter offered those results on a rental basis, so anyone who was willing to see me was willing to at least discuss the idea. And if they decided the answer was 'no,' perhaps they knew someone else who might go for the idea. Or they were impressed enough by my achievement to want to meet me just in case a job opened up.

Q: But doesn't this kind of specialized summary run the risk of coming across as overqualified?

A: I have come to believe that that's the essential weakness of every resume that is written without prior knowledge of the criteria. That kind of resume says, "This is who I am. Is that what you want?" Whereas this summary of skills says, "I understand from you that this is what you want done. Here's proof that I can do it." Besides, we're not at the point where we're talking job, work or money, so what is it that I would be over-qualified for?

It was then that some smart-ass who had been carefully studying my summary engaged me in the following dialogue. It started out by annoying me and finished with my thanking him:

Q: How do you know how well your skills went down with your contact?

A: After I had the list finished, I reviewed it, one criterion at a time. And each time I asked a test question, like, "How does that compare with what you had in mind?" I made notes on my yellow pad, so when I wrote the summary I had approval for everything I put down.

Q: Are you telling us that all the experience you recounted was exactly what your contact had in mind?

A: If I was off base, I was corrected. When that happened, I had to make note of the correction and change my summary. In this case, I was stressing my research skills, but my contact said (referring to my yellow pad) *What I'm on the lookout for is the kind of thinking that can assess the problem just by looking at the results we're getting—without waiting for input from anyone—including me.* So I changed my summary to what you see there.

Q: What do you suppose your contact meant by the term, 'on the lookout?'

A: There you have me. The straight answer is I haven't the vaguest idea because I didn't ask. I just didn't pick up on it and I'm thankful that you did. Now that I think of it, it probably wasn't the only one. But I'm following up, and I'll work out a way of dealing with that—you can bet on it.

Part 19:
Getting closer to getting work by following up.

When I was working, my own mail, on any given day, consisted of some trade periodicals, a batch of memos that either ordered, corrected or accounted for some change in plan, and bookkeeping—the invoices, purchase orders and expense vouchers that were always late. But a friendly, personal note? Never. That's why I sent this one:

Dear Contact:

Thank you for your generosity during our meeting last Thursday. I'm grateful for the information you gave me concerning the criteria by which the (aftermarket industry) would seek outside sources to get the kind of results I described. My thanks also for your suggestion that I contact (Referral) at (Company name).

I found our discussion of the need for strong team management particularly helpful. You'll recall that I added it to your list of criteria. As you can see by the enclosed summary of our conversation, I've made it a highlight. Is this the kind of skill you had in mind? In the same way, I'd welcome your comments on my revised definition of 'quick study.' Is this more in line with your thinking?

I'd appreciate any constructive comments. I could drop by for a few minutes or talk with you on the phone—whichever would be more convenient. If you can think of anyone else who should see this summary, please save the names. When I see you or call, I'll collect them.

As you suggested, I'll get in touch with (Referral) and pass on your regards. If I may, I'll report what happens.

Thanks again.

Sincerely

I wasn't kidding myself. Despite my best efforts, *productive* contacts might be few and far between. And, if it turned out that I wanted work from a number of them, I would need as many as I could get—and keep. That's why this letter was designed to keep the contact involved with me.

The secret to whatever success I had depended on how well I expanded my circle of contacts. My first source was people who would ask me how I was getting on with my job hunt. I don't know about you, but if the constant repetition of that question hasn't as yet gotten on your nerves, you don't have any. And if, like me, you're out of work and have a desperate need to find some, being nervous about it can sap your confidence. So how to handle the anxieties of well-wishers? It's easy enough to say that their anxieties are their problem. And nobody wants to be rude to family or friends. So I began to answer that question with a question of my own:

Me: Since you brought up my job-search, let me ask you: Who do you know that I can talk to in the field of (computer science, insurance, laser holography, animal husbandry, retailing, etc)?

Those who really wanted to help me stopped asking questions about how I was doing and started giving me names I could contact. Those who didn't…well, nothing gave me breathing room quite as fast as asking them for help.

Of course, the best leads to referrals are those I got as a result of a Contact Conversation. But a word of warning. What I did not want—or at least I learned later on that I did not want it—was when my contact wished to do me the 'favor' of sending my summary on to someone else on my behalf. Sounds wonderful, right? I thought so, too. But it didn't work out for a number of reasons.

First and foremost, it was pretty rare that any two of my mentors agreed on exactly the same criteria. Some concentrated more on the tools. Some concentrated more on the management problems. Some were systems people who thought they knew it all and were more interested in someone who could do the mop-up work or the details of the documentation. Sending them the summary of a meeting they hadn't attended wasn't very effective. You really had to have been there.

This was particularly true if the contact was sending the summary to his/her superior. Since the boss had not read my original letter, the summary of the result didn't tell the complete story. Further, unless the relationship between my contact and the superior was truly collegial, this confusion created a negative atmosphere for my follow up.

It wasn't much better if the recipient was a subordinate. So much time was spent in defensive questioning about why the boss had sent this along; there was little opportunity to start over.

Because 'starting over' proved to be the best way to go with every name I got. I found it much more effective to thank my contact for the offer to send the summary on, but then say something like:

Me: You've been so generous with your time as it is, please let me do it for you. Is it all right if I use your name when I contact him/her?

Then I would literally start over with my Contact Communication. Thanks to the personal referral, this time my letter read:

Dear Referred Contact,

Personal regards from (Original Contact)! Your name came up while we were discussing the criteria by which your industry might outsource the kind of results I've achieved: such as a reporting accuracy level jump by more than half, with a compliance rate improvement from 71% to near 100%.

What started our discussion was a time/cost/result analysis I made of a project to train and motivate 24 regional management teams to submit more timely and accurate performance reports for 6 headquarters worldwide.

To get it done on budget and on time, my staff and I designed and implemented secure and restricted pages on the corporate website. The regional managers' page prompted for and accepted submissions of reports, using an Excel spreadsheet template that was designed to facilitate entering complete and accurate data. A Visual Basic application at Central MIS checked them for accuracy, integrated them into a SQL Server database and returned them to the senders. Not only did the accuracy level jump by more than half, but, as I have pointed out, the compliance rate among regional managers improved from 71% to near 100%.

Now, suppose, instead of hiring someone like me to achieve this improvement, aftermarket companies could *rent* results like these on a monthly, weekly or even daily basis? I'm particularly interested in organizations with a great deal of dealership data. The question I want to ask has to do with determining their criteria for outsourcing results similar to the one I've described. Is Thursday OK? I'll call you the day before to set a time. If that's not convenient, will you leave word with your assistant about the best time to get together?

Thanks, Contact, I appreciate your guidance.

Signed

I saved a lot of creative time by not reinventing the wheel. Whenever a paragraph worked once, I tried it again—and again. Go with a winner, that's me. And I didn't overlook the personal aspect of the communication. If it looked personal, the message was most likely to get through.

Part 20:
Follow the yellow brick road

Who wouldn't want a sure way to find what it was they were looking for, and the easier the road, the better? And there are certainly enough wizards around to tell you what to do or to even do it for you—for a nonrefundable fee. I found that while getting work is work, helping people to get work is a business. That's why each mentor I found was so valuable. They cost me nothing but effort—of which I was ready to supply plenty. They gave me the rules of the game for their particular business or industry so that I could compete on a level playing field. But most important, they gave me my confidence back. I found that I could meet almost all the criteria they gave me. That's why I made sure they knew how much their information meant to me when I mailed the summary of our conversation.

Thank you for your generosity during our meeting last Thursday.

This is a reminder to whatever guardian may open the mail—or my contact reading in a rush. It's a reminder of who I am and that I've been there and had a meeting.

I'm grateful for the information you gave me concerning the criteria by which the (aftermarket industry) would seek outside sources to get the kind of results I described.

This is more than a reminder since it sums up the topic of our conversation. What it really says is that I lived up to my promise and didn't crowd you for a job. I can be trusted not to crowd you in future.

My thanks also for your suggestion that I contact (Referral) at (Company.)

You were sufficiently impressed by my skills to give me a referral.

I found our discussion of the need for strong team management particularly helpful. You'll recall that I added it to your list of criteria. As you can see by the enclosed summary of our conversation, I've made it a highlight. Is this the kind of skill you had in mind? In the same way, I'd welcome your comments on my revised definition of 'quick study.' Is this more in line with your thinking?

We discussed a number of criteria. Why did I choose this one to highlight? Because while you hadn't made 'strong team management' part of your original list, I made note of what you said in response to my 'how about' question: *Stron-*

ger yet when you're an outsider and the team's inside. What were you telling me—that you might consider it if you could be sure about how well an outsider like me could manage your inside team?

That outsider/insider problem seemed to be only one possible source of concern. We also talked about the importance of being a 'quick study,' which you found worth defining in terms of what you were on the lookout for. I failed to talk more about that at the time. I'd welcome another opportunity.

I'd appreciate any constructive comments. I could drop by for a few minutes or talk with you on the phone—whichever would be more convenient.

Now that our conversation is down on paper and you've had a chance to study it, what kind of impression has it made? If you can think of anyone else who should see this summary, please save the names and when I see you or call, I'll collect them.

As you suggested, I'll get in touch with (Referral) and pass on your regards. If I may, I'll report what happens.

Yet another good reason to stay in touch. If my referral agrees to see me, it means he thinks well of my contact. If he thinks well of my contact, he'll say nice things. Here is my chance to pass them along.

Bottom line, all I want is a chance to talk a bit more. What about? A number of topics come to mind:

Is there some project that's in trouble?

Is there something that's happening that management doesn't want to be happening?

Is there something that management wants to be happening that isn't happening?

No harm in just discussing the possibilities, right? For all my contact knows, I've got an answer. Or I can come up with one—one that will save time, save money, save man-hours and make my contact look good? I've done it for others. Can I do it for him/her? Perhaps. Perhaps not. The only way to make sure would be to talk about it.

If you can think of anyone else who should see this summary, please save the names and when I see you or call, I'll collect them.

As you suggested, I'll get in touch with (Referral) and pass on your regards.

Just to prove there's no pressure on you, I'm prepared to go elsewhere. Since you suggested the referral, there's a good chance you know others in the field.

If I may, I'll report what happens. Thanks again.

I have a backup reason for keeping in touch.

Part 21:
Show me the money.

First, the good news. Whenever I did the work, wrote a good paragraph, did persistent follow-up and asked the right question of the right person, I learned enough about the criteria to accurately direct the summary of my skills and experience to my target organization or industry. I felt that this put me on the inside track. While it did not mean automatic success, it did mean I had learned *how*. And once I knew how, I became convinced that success would be a matter of persistence.

Now, the bad news. There were times when I said or did the wrong things. Or I failed to say or do enough of the right things. Not deliberately. The last thing in the word I wanted to do was to shoot myself in the foot. But sometimes I did. Nervousness perhaps—or the contact was so important that I deserted the very ideas that got me face to face in the first place. This didn't mean I was a bad person or that I had no talent or was a loser. It meant that, under stress, I had made a mistake. Mistakes are there to be reviewed and corrected.

But whenever I heard myself saying things like "I didn't get through because they or he or she…" I whispered softly to myself in a way that would not offend sensitive ears: "Bullshit." I was just laying it off. I was letting myself off the hook—which was like letting the steam out of my anger. Instead, I channeled my resentment at having been ignored into an even greater determination to break through. What was it I could have done better…with more accuracy…with more effort? It was there, somewhere.

I brought this up because I was reviewing what I considered to be a job interview—except that I refused to call it by that name. I refused as a matter of definition. To me a job interview is when there is a job open that has been:

Circulated throughout the company so that many insiders know about it and wish to apply or to tip off their friends.

Advertised or posted on the job sites so that there are at least a thousand resumes fighting for attention.

Assigned to a headhunter who will pass along my resume along with the others but will recommend the applicant who is under eleven years of age.

Designed to take advantage of the present competition by asking for too much while paying too little.

I, on the other hand, learned not to chase after job openings. If I saw a good listing that presented a clear range of criteria that I thought I could meet, I wouldn't answer it. Instead, I would research the company that placed the ad, get some management names and quotes I could use and send a Contact Communication. If there was no company name I would write a resume that responded to the listed criteria just for the exercise—and then forget about it.

Of course, if the job opening came flying toward me, I didn't duck. As I think I've already pointed out, whenever the contact referred to some situation within his or her own organization, using phrases like 'speaking for us' or 'we ourselves,' the discussion changed. What I was hearing was not a general view of the industry. What I was hearing were the criteria for a position my contact was hoping to get management to approve. Or, management may have already approved it, but the search had not yet begun.

As I have already said, the advantage of initiating this conversation put me first in line. I had it front-loaded for success, because there was no competition. I wasn't on anybody's short list because there wasn't any list. There had been no ads, no postings, not even a rumor. So how did I blow it? Let me begin at the beginning.

One of my contacts liked my summary so much that when I called to follow up she told me she was going to send it on to the MIS in one of their divisions. They had been running into some problems of late that she felt I might help to resolve. No guarantee, of course. While the guy in charge was technically his subordinate, she had a thing about micromanaging. She would send him my summary with a note making clear that the decision would be his.

Remember how I said this sounded like a wonderful idea, but it wasn't? Not only did my bad experience warn me, but the social worker in me immediately flashed on what would happen in the mind of the subordinate the moment that communication crossed his desk. While there was an outside chance that he'd welcome his boss's help, it was too far outside for me to risk. I could just see him looking for reasons to reject what would come across to him as her attempt to influence his thinking. After all, my summary was a response to *her* thinking. What was *his* thinking? Would he, for example, take it as a criticism from a superior—an inference that he couldn't cut it? Was I going to be his replacement?

If I could make contact with him first, find out what was on his mind, sell him on my value on a just-between-us basis (and save the heavy guns for just-in-case) it would be his decision. So, as I had learned how the hard way, I thanked her profusely. I pointed out that she had already been more than generous with her time and effort. I promised that if she would just give me the particulars, I'd be happy to take it from there. She did, and I did. This time my letter read:

Dear Referral,

Personal regards from (Original Contact! Your name came up while we were discussing the criteria by which your industry might outsource the kind of results I've achieved: such as a reporting accuracy level jump by more than half, with a compliance rate improvement from 71% to near 100%. She was generous enough to give me her list of criteria and suggested that your current needs might suggest some important additions.

The project we reviewed was one in which...(My original paragraphs followed. Only the end of the letter was a bit different.)

I explained that, instead of hiring someone like me to achieve this improvement, aftermarket companies could *rent* results like these on a monthly, weekly or even daily basis. That's what started our discussion of the criteria for outsourcing results similar to the one I've described. In line with her suggestion, I'd like to review her list with you and get your additions. Is Thursday OK? I'll call you the day before to set a time. If that's not convenient, will you leave word with your assistant about the best time to get together?

Thanks, Referral, I appreciate your guidance.

By sending a letter instead of a summary of our Contact Conversation it seemed like I was starting from the beginning. In truth, I was. Would I have done the same if I had been told there was an actual opening and that her subordinate was currently on a search? In retrospect, I think so. My reasoning was that I had no idea of the relationship between the two parties. I only knew how I would feel if my ex-boss had tried to push his candidate on me back when I was hiring. I didn't want one of those my-boss-says-to-see-you-so-I-will interviews. I'll admit that the moment I dropped my letter in the mail, I had second thoughts. I felt like I was getting off the yellow brick road. But the last thing in the world I wanted to happen was for my contact to energize her subordinate into putting the job on the market. That's why I made clear this was just a suggestion. To make it crystal clear, I mentioned it twice:

She was generous enough to give me her list of criteria and suggested that your current needs might suggest some important additions.

In line with her suggestion, I'd like to review her list with you and get your additions.

That way I hoped I wouldn't be competing with a bunch of other people. I planned to be there ahead of them. Or even *instead* of them.

Part 22:
The DOW (Discussion Of Work)

What could go wrong? I had been tipped off—a situation existed that called for my skills. I was ahead of the curve—this would be a discussion about getting work that had not yet been listed, advertised or posted. I was feeling no stress—despite the fact that I needed the work—because I knew that I would be spared one of those painfully sad endings. "We have other people to see." "We'll review all the applicants and let you know." And the all-time favorite, "We'll call you Thursday at the latest." There was no one else. It was me, or nothing.

As it turned out, it was nothing. My fault, too.

Were you a fly on the wall, you'd never guess the ending from the way it began. Instead of the usual awkward moments of meeting a stranger and breaking the ice, I had already set the stage for this meeting. I just referred to my letter:

Me:	As I explained in my letter, I had a meeting with Joan Contact (who sends her best, by the way). She was kind enough to tell me her criteria for getting work in this industry and suggested you might have information to add. I have her list right here. May I take just a few moments to review it?
They:	Sure. I'm curious about what she had to say.

CRITERIA	
THE TOOLS	EXCEL, SPREAD - SHEETS, WEB PAGE DESIGN, ETC
A QUICK STUDY	HOW OPS MGT USES DATA
ABILITY TO PUT TOGETHER A ROBUST SYSTEM	RUN FAILURE-FREE WITHOUT TWEAKING & Mgt AGGRAVATION
KNOW-HOW TO DESIGN REPORTS VERY	ANSWER QUESTIONS VS.PROVOKING THEM
A ~~DAMN~~ GOOD COMMUNICATOR	MUST INTERFACE WITH INSIDE PEOPLE IN OTHER DEPARTMENTS
TIME AND MONEY	NO BUDGETS FOR EMERGENCIES
STRONG TEAM MANAGER	YOU'RE AN OUTSIDER AND THE TEAM'S INSIDE
ABILITY TO TRAIN THE TRAINERS	NOT HERE - BUT AT ACME PARTS?

As we reviewed the list, I began to get the sense that ours was a discussion rather than an interview. At first, that idea discouraged me. I hadn't done all that work just to have a chat. But then my thinking went into overdrive. Why did this guy agree to meet with me? Was it to appease his boss? Or was something about what I had to say of sufficient interest for him to at least give it a shot? Since, in his mind, he had no openings as such, why *should* this be a formal interview? Why not just a discussion of the work, a meeting of the minds, during which his needs and my needs get together? I thought I would get a pretty good idea from the way he answered my question:

Me:	Would you have any criteria to add to this list? Are there any that shouldn't be there?
They:	We use a few more tools than she mentioned, but for someone who's a quick study, that's no big thing. I can't think of anything that shouldn't be there, but there are some pretty significant items that I think should be added.
Me:	Then let's do that, shall we? Let's add them to the list.
They:	I'm not sure it can be expressed in a few neat words, but I'm constantly after my people not to dump every problem in my lap and then wait for my instructions to do something they feel has to be done. Get after it—and then tell me what, when and why.
Me:	That was once called 'being a self-starter,' but we live in a more sophisticated time. How about we call it something like RESPONSIVE THINKING AND ACTION.
They:	Good enough.
Me:	Let me add it to the list. Is there anything else?
They:	I'm not sure how to express it as a criterion—but you'd have to be invisible.
Me:	INVISIBLE. Let me add that to the list, though I must admit I don't fully understand it.
They:	Our department has a head-count freeze right now, and there's no telling how long it will last. If I dropped someone to bring fresh talent aboard, I could lose that someone without gaining another head. It's part of a plan to reduce overhead.

Me:	So the criterion would be, DON'T ADD TO THE HEAD-COUNT. Does that say it?
They:	(Laughs) That's what the memo from upstairs said—almost word for word. And I'm short-handed as it is. But who isn't? We still have to catch up on a lot of documentation…. accurate documentation.
Me:	Since you stressed the word 'accurate,' let me include it. WRITE ACCURATE DOCUMENTATION. Is there anything else?
They:	(With a touch of sarcasm) Yes. Getting people to work together more effectively—as a team, rather than as competitive individuals. The job market being what it is, everybody is focused on holding on to their own bit of space. I'm not sure how you'd describe that on your list.
Me:	How about the ability to MOTIVATE TEAM PER-FORMANCE. Does that say it, do you think?
They:	I like it because it doesn't blame anybody.
Me:	OK, let's review what we've added:

RESPONSIVE	
THINKING	
& ACTION	
INVISIBLE	DON'T ADD TO
	HEAD COUNT
WRITE ACCURATE	
DOCUMENTATION	
MOTIVATE TEAM	
PERFORMANCE	

I called this a Discussion Of Work rather than a job interview for the usual three reasons:

First, there was no actual job opening. True, his immediate boss said there was a need. For all I knew, she had passed that word on to him—including the fact that I'd be in touch. In any event, he had expressed a number of needs.

Second, I was looking for work rather than a job—which was just as well since management was in the midst of a cost-reduction program and against adding any head-count.

Third was the difference in the nature of the communication. If this had been a typical job interview, I would have been telling about myself and he would have been listening. In a Discussion Of Work, however, both of us were involved. My contact was explaining his needs and I was getting ready to respond with my ability to fill them. When I judged that he had finished adding to my list, I was ready to take my S-H-O-T:

Me:	We agreed on *responsive thinking and action* as a way of avoiding the problems getting dumped in your lap while people wait for your instruction.
	This reminds me of *a situation where one of our programs turned out to be not as robust as originally thought* and no amount of tweaking was making it right. An interdepartmental crisis was on the way with everyone blaming everyone else. My thinking was, "Let's fix the problem, not the blame. I had a solution in mind, but I lacked the authority to summon the other people to a meeting and didn't want to dump the problem in management's lap. So I contacted one of those custom T-shirt places and ordered a half-dozen in dark blue with white lettering that read, "Don't fix the blame..." on the front and "Fix the problem" on the back. I dropped them off at each desk with a memo suggesting that we get together for lunch on the next dress-down day. Everyone showed wearing the shirt and everyone got with the program.
	Here's the group picture we took when we had our celebratory lunch. I happen to have it with me. The rolled-up paper each of them is holding is the 'attaboy' the team got from top management. Notice who's missing from the picture? Me. For two reasons: First, I was

taking the picture. Second, I wanted to be invisible and make sure they got the credit.

This seems to relate the kind of responsive thinking and action you added to the list, but to be sure, let me ask: *How does this compare with the think-and-act criterion you had in mind?*

They: Yes. That ties in. If you have a few minutes, tell me what the problem was and how you went about solving it.

If *I* had a few minutes? Riiiiiight! What followed was a technical Q&A and we never did get to the other criteria. Pretty soon we were knee-deep into his current situation and I was asking questions about his problems with the quality of the documentation as if we were colleagues.

Needless to say, I spent a lot of time rethinking and recapping what had happened and why. I certainly didn't have a tape recorder going, so the notes I took during and immediately after our discussion were all I had to go by. Here's how I analyzed what happened and why:

When I first started looking for work, I would wait for the decision-maker to set the tone of our meeting. This was a particularly awkward moment for both of us—particularly if he or she really had no opening and was seeing me on the charitable insistence of third party. It was even worse for me if there *was* an opening and they were looking for someone younger. Then, despite the fact that I was right there, they literally stopped seeing me. I learned to recognize that drop of the eyes that put us out of contact, and that disappointed expression that told me everything without a word being said. I wondered afterward if I sounded as angry as I was.

Here's another way I put my anger to work. My new mantra was: There is no opening and I have nothing to lose, so I would take charge and set the tone:

As I explained in my letter, I had a meeting with Joan Contact (who sends her best, by the way). She was kind enough to tell me her criteria for getting work in this industry and suggested you might have information to add. I have her list right here. May I take just a few moments to review it?

Now I had a tool to work with—that list of criteria. Furthermore, I had a name to drop. But I still asked for permission to proceed with a review of the list. If he were at all interested, he would have something to add. And he did.

I'm constantly after my people not to dump every problem in my lap and then wait for my instructions to do something they feel has to be done. Get after it—and then tell me what, when and why.

I didn't need a background in social work to sense that if someone is 'constantly' trying to achieve a particular result, that result must be evading him. I could have taken that as my cue to jump in with a, "Hey! I'm the guy you need!" But I had learned to resist the impulse, remember? Instead, I clarified his interpretation of that criterion by highlighting an experience in my own career:

An important program turned out to be not as robust as originally thought and no amount of tweaking was making it right. An interdepartmental crisis was on the way with everyone blaming everyone else. My thinking was, "Let's fix the problem, not the blame," and I had a solution in mind. I lacked the authority to summon the other people to a meeting and didn't want to dump the problem in management's lap.

I was careful to build my story around the phrase he had used: *I'm constantly after my people not to dump every problem in my lap.* That way I felt I could relate it directly to his need. If it sounds like I had learned to adlib, nothing could be further from the truth. What I did do, in order to compensate for the fact that I cannot speak to smoothly 'off the top of my head,' was to prepare a brief presentation for each of the criteria Joan Contact had given me. To save time, I used the same outline of selecting the criterion and highlighting some experience. Then it was time to offer evidence of success:

Here's the group picture we took when we had our celebratory lunch. I happen to have it with me. The rolled-up paper each of them is holding is the 'attaboy' the team got from top management. Notice who's missing from the picture? Me. For two reasons: First, I was taking the picture. Second, I wanted to be invisible and make sure they got the credit.

By showing the photograph I 'happened to have' with me. I figured that someone with interdepartmental problems might react positively to those smiling faces and the attaboy memos in everybody's hand—and relate it to his need for the kind of responsive thinking and action he had added to the list. And I didn't forget the invisibility.

Then it was time for a reality check with a test question: how accurately did my presentation meet the criterion?

"How does this compare with the think-and-act criterion you had in mind?

How could I have missed? He was coming through with all the right questions and I was coming through with all the right answers. But before we even got to the part where I ask him to show me the money, he's thanking me for coming, telling me he's going to give our discussion some serious thought and walking me out. I didn't even get the chance to thank him for his time and ask if there were any other people I should talk to. There he was, smiling at me as the elevator door slid shut, leaving me with the feeling he had just sold me a used car.

As far as the Discussion Of Work was concerned, the DOW had just hit rock bottom.

Part 23:
Closing the deal.

Sounds pretty tacky, doesn't it? That is a term a salesman might draw on to describe that critical moment in the negotiation where everybody is smiling but nobody is buying. Tacky or not, that's what happened to me. Why? In hopes of finding the answer I went over and over my notes. I wrote out the discussion as clearly as I could recall it and studied every important phase and phrase. But I couldn't find anything I had done wrong.

To the contrary. Knowing my weaknesses in talking about me, I had prepared. I felt confident—not because it was a cliché I had picked up in that church basement, but because I had verified there was a market for my skills. I even sounded confident because I had practiced saying what I had written. I mean I practiced aloud—full volume. I just had to get accustomed to the idea of presenting myself in a way that would make a positive impression. I admit I felt a little foolish—particularly when my daughter came into the den and asked who I was talking to. Coward that I am, I told her I was just thinking out loud. The lie was so transparent that I couldn't imagine what she was thinking. What she said was, "You sounded pretty good." I took it as a compliment, but from then on I saved my rehearsals for when I was alone.

In any event, after a lot of study, I was sure I had figured out what went wrong. It wasn't something I did. It wasn't something my contact did. It was something I had failed to do. More important, it was my second failure. OK, perhaps 'failure' is a harsh term, but how else would you describe the failure—I can't think of any better term—to respond to an expressed need?

That's very good, but it's not quite what I had in mind when I said 'quick study.' What I'm on the lookout for is the kind of thinking that can assess the problem just by looking at the results we're getting—without waiting for input from anyone—including me.

How might I have responded instead of saying thank-you and goodbye? Suppose instead I had said:

Me:	According to my notes, you said earlier that you were on the lookout for the kind of thinking that can asses a problem just by looking at the results. How did you mean the term, 'on the lookout?'

There might have been any number of possible answers to that question:

They:	Any manager has to be on the lookout to improve departmental performance.
They:	That was just an expression I used at a staff meeting just this week.
They:	Well, since you ask, I put in for another head-count. Hiring freeze or not, the work has to get done.
They:	I'm not getting enough of that from some of my outside sources.

Now, then, which of these answers would have suggested a possible opportunity? All of them. Which of these answers did I get? None of them, because of my failure—that word again—to ask the question. "*How did you mean…?*"

I didn't ask it because I hadn't prepared it, so I wasn't as well prepared as I thought—not only to ask the question, but to be ready for the possible answers. What I needed was a response that would move any of the above reactions toward a productive closure. The one I came up with—a little too late—was a three-parter::

Me:	What project were you thinking of?

My thinking was that if I get a project description at this point, I'm halfway home.

Me:	When may I get a look at what you're describing?

Any walk-through or paperwork has me rounding third.

Me:	How soon do you need this completed?

The nearer the deadline, the higher the score.

Naturally, this is the oldie but goldie about avoiding questions that can be answered 'yes' or 'no' by beginning them with 'what,' 'when,' 'why,' and 'how.' That meant the discussion would continue, with the strong possibility that our Discussion of Work would lead to work and the DOW would zoom. But I blew it—and had only myself to blame.

Part 24:
Putting anger to work.

How about when the person I'm angriest at is me? Not just because I wasted a couple of great opportunities, but because of something that went a lot deeper. Simply put, *I had not prepared for success because I didn't really expect to be successful.* It took me a while to write that thought—that admission, really—but now that it was on paper, I had to deal with it. Where did that sense of defeat come from? Was it the way so many of my friends and colleagues backed away when I got the push? Was it my wife Cheryl's uncertainty when I disclosed my plan? Was it the prevailing attitude of the long-term unemployed that permeated the church basement? Or was it, in truth, all these weeks of my own failure that had ground me down?

Whatever the cause, I found myself at an important crossroad: choosing between embarrassment and anger. Do I let my failure loom so large that it becomes an impossible obstacle, or do I go back to these people and ask for another chance—using my anger at myself as a self-punishing propellant? True, I never heard of it being done, but I knew of no law against it.

Dear (First Name of initial contact)

Excuse the informality, but after our discussion I feel we know each other well enough for me to make a confession. I think I missed a cue. It happened while you were correcting my definition of your criterion, 'quick study.' According to my notes (copy enclosed) you said it was not quite what you had in mind. "What I'm on the lookout for," you explained, "is the kind of thinking that can assess the problem just by looking at the results we're getting—without waiting for input from anyone—including me."

The temptation to interrupt you was so strong and I was so focused on what I could hardly wait to say, that I wasn't listening as carefully as I should have.

Can I have another chance? I need just enough time to ask 3 quick questions. We could do it on the phone, but as you will see, face to face would be far more productive and would take about the same amount of time.

This Thursday or Friday? Any time you say. I'll check with Wendy, OK?

Thank you for allowing me to throw myself on your mercy.

Now who, in his or her right mind would write that kind of letter? More important, who has ever gotten a letter like that? If I wasn't so pissed off at me, I would have been much too self-conscious to even think those thoughts—much less put them on paper. I forget who it was who said confession is good for the soul. I'm not too sure about that, but my main concern was whether or not confession was good for another appointment. I was throwing myself on the mercy of my contact—and said as much:

Dear (First Name)

Excuse the informality, but after our discussion I feel we know each other well enough for me to make a confession: I think I missed a cue.

Always conscious of the Guardian at the Gate, I allowed myself the luxury of a first-name relationship—whether it actually developed or not. Besides, it fit the tone of this letter.

It happened while you were correcting my definition of your criterion: 'quick study.' According to my notes (copy enclosed) you said it was not quite what you had in mind.

Perhaps she remembered, perhaps not. That's why I included a photocopy of my notes.

"What I'm on the lookout for," you explained, "is the kind of thinking that can assess the problem just by looking at the results we're getting—without waiting for input from anyone—including me."

There was a whole lot of iffy discussion in my group when the topic of taking notes came up. There were implications of everything from it being awkward to a sign of disrespect. The one that got a lot of us laughing was the accusation that note-taking slowed down the interview. Do we really want to rush through the precious time we have face to face? But most important, if I did get work from her, wouldn't I make careful notes during any assignment?

The temptation to interrupt you was so strong, and I was so focused on what I could hardly wait to say, that I wasn't listening as carefully as I should have.

OK, so it sounded a little dramatic, but I had to explain the lapse in my usual quick thinking. The best lie to tell was the truth.

Can I have another chance? I need just enough time to ask 3 quick questions. We could do it on the phone, but as you will see, face to face would be far more productive and would take about the same amount of time.

The three questions I worked out could be asked on the phone, but the most important answer involves what was happening—or not happening—over there.

This Thursday or Friday? Any time you say. I'll check with Wendy, OK?

I included the name of the guardian because I made a note of it. Putting her into the picture could mean a lot when I called.

Thank you for allowing me to throw myself on your mercy.

As I said before, that was precisely what I was doing.

Somebody else once said, "In for a penny, in for a pound." I was in for 37 cents. So how about twice that amount with a second letter:

Dear (First Name of referral),

Excuse the informality, but after our discussion I feel we know each other well enough for me to make a confession: I think I missed a cue. It happened while you were explaining (as per the enclosed notes) your need to get people to work together more effectively—as a team, rather than competitive individuals because, as you worded it, "We have to catch up on a lot of documentation…. accurate documentation."

Our discussion of fixing the problem without fixing blame had me so intrigued and I was so focused on answering your questions that I may not have been listening as carefully as I should have.

Can I have another chance? I need just enough time to ask 3 quick questions. We could do it on the phone, but as you will see, face to face would be far more productive and would take about the same amount of time.

This Thursday or Friday? Any time you say. I'll check with (Assistant), OK?

Thank you for allowing me to throw myself on your mercy.

And both did.

Part 25:
The contact is at risk, too.

The whole event was quite a contrast to the opportunities I blew earlier in my search, before I learned the *shouldas*. Instead of delivering a fascinating, 30-minute lecture on the subject of "Every Detail Of My Working Life From The Very Beginning" I *shoulda* focused on the criteria the contact felt had to be met and how to persuade him or her that I was the one with the skills needed to meet them. I clearly remember how, as I waited, I was only too aware that the rest of my working life might well hang on these next few minutes. No matter how hard I tried to reduce my stress level by reciting such positive ideas as "life goes on" and "this isn't the end of the world," that tension was still there.

Other people may work best under that kind of pressure. Well, good for them. But to me, interpersonal situations were a real problem. I was so aware of my own discomfort that I wasn't really focused on what the other party to the discussion might be experiencing. It took me a number of encounters to figure it out, but I finally learned how to hear the cues that indicated just how much stress my contact was under.

I even took the precaution to get to the site of our meeting with 30 minutes to spare. I made it clear to the reception person that I didn't wish to be announced yet, so that I could use the time to organize my materials and put on my game face.

Most important, I had time to review my material: the letter I had sent to set up the first contact, the list of criteria, the summary of our previous conversation and the three questions I planned to ask. But as the time for our encounter drew near, what, if anything, was my contact thinking? It wasn't too long ago that I, too, had a job that was loaded with responsibility and a plate that was overloaded with work. So I should know. It was a pretty good bet that he/she was under pressure to improve productivity, profit, efficiency, and find solutions to problems that might even facilitate a promotion. Or else.

Or else what? Or else they might wind up where I am—on the wrong side of the desk. I must confess that it never occurred to me, until I got fired, that every day I showed up for work *I* was at risk. Of course I was aware of my responsibilities—everybody who works for a living has to answer to somebody. Why else was I always hoping there was no phone message awaiting me that demanded an immediate meeting with my boss? But I never thought of it in those terms. I do now.

Responsibility is something that everybody has to somebody. Whatever decision is made, responsibility to superiors for the quality of that decision is pretty obvious. If there *was* an opportunity for work with this organization, would my contact want someone who looked like me to fill it? Or would he or she anticipate some difficulty getting management approval...a difficulty that involved risk? Could that be why she didn't come up with an offer the first time around?

If there was no opening as such—just the problems that needed to be solved—would adding someone like me, even on a temporary basis, create other problems? What if I outperformed members of the regular staff? This would require more decisions to be made. These are the kinds of decisions that could risk dissension. Dissension could spread the message that my contact wasn't much of a manager. Why did she tolerate that poor performer in the first place?

Which is where indecision rears its ugly head. Does my contact take what appears to be the safe route for now and do nothing? Or is doing nothing really all that safe? Is it better to ignore my existence or take me on? Then, if I succeed, I'm invisible and my contact gets the credit. If I don't succeed, I suddenly become visible and get all the blame.

Or will my contact persuade management that I'm the person best suited to help achieve the objectives they have in mind? That sounds logical. But what if my age, sex, color, personality, height, weight and previous condition of servitude didn't mesh with the profile? Image is what was at stake. Those who believe they are what they eat or they are what they wear have nothing on the organizations that feel they are whom they employ. My contact can be stuck with "how it looks," and that can influence the final decision.

How will it look if my contact has someone fifteen years her senior reporting to her? True, someone with my depth of experience could help this organization compete more successfully, but that would be in the long term. What if there is more concern with how I would make the organization look today than how I can help it to look in the future?

Which is why the knowledge of every phase of the job but how to interview is such a handicap to making the most productive decision. The sad fact is that most of the people who rise to Decision-Maker rank because they have been trained to do their respective jobs so well, fail to see interviewing as the kind of skill that also requires training. I sure didn't realize that when I was on the inside making those decisions.

Nor did I appreciate that looking for work was also a discipline that had to be mastered. Planning? Preparation? Practice? Nothing could have been further from my mind. I went into this effort flying absolutely blind. This meant that during this all-important process, which may have decided my future and that of the decision-maker, the matter rested in the hands of two amateurs—one on each side of the desk:

As a problem-solver, why hadn't I figured all that out right at the start?

Better late than never. Here's what I've learned since. No one looking for work is the perfect choice. As I looked around that church basement, it became obvious that for one reason or another, none of us were ideal candidates. Some, like me, were too old. Put as brave a face on it as you like, the stats tell the story. The over-fifties were having one heck of a time. Some of us had jobs that, over time, had simply disappeared. They aren't needed any more. By focusing on those jobs rather than on the skills needed to do the work, these people wound up searching for something that no longer exists. So some had given up—and it showed. They came to these meetings as their weekly social hour and had nothing to contribute but an air of defeat.

No job is perfect, either. That's why I moved from looking for employment to looking for the kind of work that met *my* criteria: the opportunity to utilize my skills for the best possible buck. It would be only honest to admit that some work demanded criteria I couldn't meet. I could, as I explain later on, negotiate my way around practically all of them. Except my age. That was non-negotiable. So I had to turn it into an asset. Here's how:

Years ago, when I started to work, it seemed that everyone expected to hire dedicated, hard-working, job-oriented people who know how to perform within company policy and complete the work on time. No doubt I saw myself as a dedicated, hard-working, job-oriented person who knew how to perform within company policy and complete the work on time. Wasn't everybody? But then, how is it that some people wound up carrying more of the load because some of their colleagues habitually came in late, left early, or took lunch-hours that were really mini-vacations? What made the situation even more complex was the way management reacted. Instead of listing these important work-habits as part of the job criteria, they let them "go without saying." Then, after it was too late because the wrong person had been hired, they came up with warnings or incentives to correct the situation.

Hard to believe? I don't recall exactly when they introduced the "personal day." Those who are convinced that people who tell lies don't get into heaven also believe that angels invented the personal day to make it unnecessary for perfectly healthy people to call in sick. On any given day, in ballparks, movie theaters or just at home waiting for the plumber, are roughly a gazillion wage earners not earning their wages.

But that was then. This is now. So I figured it would be to my advantage to make what usually goes without saying, actually said. Sure, I'm older. It means that when I went to school, we were still being taught how to write an English sentence that recognized the importance of spelling, punctuation and grammar. It means I have older work habits. I show up. I know how to listen. I take accurate notes. I deliver accurate results.

What goaded me into this line of thinking was what I called, "That look." It was that drop of the eyes that told me how disappointed my contact was in meeting me for the first time: balding, a few pounds overweight with an appearance you won't find in Gentlemen's Quarterly and obviously a low-energy burnout case. There were those in my group who tried to counter the impact of time with hair dye, comb-overs and clothes designed for someone twenty years younger. It didn't help them. It wouldn't have helped me. What I needed was a way of reassuring my contact that I was worth the risk of giving work to someone like me.

Now here's a funny thing: work habits were never listed as part of the criteria. Never. Did management expect every employee to show up and be as productive as possible? Of course. That went without saying. So, quite understandably, *nobody said it*. So instead of all those cosmetic weapons against age discrimination, I used a what-you-see-is-what-you-get approach. I demonstrated the advantages of my mature experience:

1. Writing the unconventional letter to set up the appointment demonstrated the fact that I was ahead of the curve. No resume and cover letter for me. That was old-fashioned.

2. The way I followed up my letter to set the appointment took energy and persistence—and more than a little planning and preparation. As work habits, these aren't just valuable—they're priceless.

3. Asking the 'criteria question' and taking careful notes of the response was totally non-traditional. Those of us who have been around the block more than once have learned to communicate. That's how I demonstrated it.

4. Summarizing the conversation rather than grinding out yet another resume was completely out of the box. There's nothing like an older head for newer thinking.

5. The very fact that I have this long a track record should be reassuring. I've not only accumulated a great deal of experience, but I have already made my mistakes—and have learned from them. Now I'm ready to go on from there.

What could sound more obvious? Small wonder nobody ever brought it up. I must admit I wouldn't have done so, either, had it not been for the fact that I was trying to cash in on my age. I learned to work at a time when standards of performance were a great deal more demanding. Nobody ever won an award for not being absent or arriving on time. That's what we did. That's what we all did. That's what I'm prepared to do now.

Part 26:
Negotiating the arrangement.

Now that I knew how I had blown it, I was back for another try. Why would any contact, as busy as they all are—be willing to give our discussion another go-round? Simple. They thought they had something to gain. Not everyone, of course, but I didn't need everyone. Looked at from the contact's side of the desk, the criteria she gave me represented a wish list for building a team that had the ability, experience and knowledge she wanted. The question in my mind that encouraged me was this:

How well did her present team meet her own criteria?

I didn't think I could get away with asking that question directly—as much as I would have liked to. These were, after all, her people. Maybe she hired them. Maybe she inherited them. Maybe she was totally satisfied. Maybe she wanted to see what else was being offered. That's where I came in.

The 'nice-to-see-you-agains' didn't take much time and set the stage for my introduction of the purpose of this meeting. The very fact that I was the one doing the introduction was another major difference between what was about to happen and the traditional job interview. In the case of the latter, it was always the decision-maker who established the procedure. That's where the whole idea of the 'sit-down-and-tell-me-about-yourself' got started. But this is different:

Me:	As I explained in my letter about our last meeting, I think I missed a cue. According to my notes you said, "What I'm on the lookout for is the kind of thinking that can assess the problem just by looking at the results we're getting—without waiting for input from anyone—including me."
They:	Well, that didn't mean I was actually on the lookout for anyone at the present time.

Me:	Understood. But I took it to mean that you wanted your people to be constantly evaluating the results you're getting and assess any problem that might arise. I had promised only three questions, so my first one is: What project or program were you thinking of?
They:	The one that's always on my mind is our branch customer/value analysis—what we call the CVA. It's a typical report, but it's a critical one because we're always test-marketing new services.
Me:	Since I'm test-marketing my services, permit me to make you a no cost, no obligation offer. As you saw in my summary, I have the background and skills to meet all your criteria. So let me make an assessment of a typical report—just to see if any improvements are called for. If I can't come up with anything that might help, you haven't lost a thing. If I do, any suggestions I make are your property. Since it's a win-win situation, when may I get a look at what you're describing?
They:	It sounds good, but I'm afraid that's proprietary information.
Me:	The same was true in my previous situation. Each of us had to sign a confidentiality agreement. When I decided to rent my skills to different organizations in the same industry, I checked with my own attorney and he provided me with the necessary form. Here it is, signed and notarized.
They:	You have given it a lot of thought. It sounds good, but I'll have to buzz it by our legal department. Have you got a few minutes?

People who are willing to talk are generally willing to listen. This did not always mean they had an immediate need for my help, but it was at least an indication of a willingness to review the possibilities I had to offer. Of course, there were those who said they were already on top of everything and were too busy or harassed to get involved. Instead of speaking my anger, like: "If you're so much on top of things how is it that you're too busy or harassed?" I used my anger as part of my strategy. That's why I kept a special trouble-shooting section in my journal for them.

And there were those who came up with criteria I simply couldn't meet. They're in that special section, too. But for the most part, if my paragraph was of interest to the contact, I got an audience. To me, that audience meant that somewhere, in the back of that contact's mind, was a need. The list of criteria gave me an indication of that need. But it didn't answer the most important question: WHEN. If convinced enough to rent or hire me, how soon would the contact be ready to make a commitment? I needed the income.

There I sat, waiting for the answer to my third question. My first got me a description of a program. My second (as it turned out) got me the paperwork—a sample of the report. My third was the key:

Me: How soon do you want me to get back to you with an assessment?

All that hung in the balance was my future. If my contact didn't really care about where or when, this report was no problem and therefore low or no priority. But then, why even bring it up? But when she said:

They: Well, how soon can you get back to me? Is Monday OK?

Bingo.

There was a time when I hated to write plans of action. Mainly because I didn't consider myself a writer. What saved me from embarrassment was my stint in the Peace Corps. To save time (and maybe paper) everything was written in pseudo-military memo form: Date; From; To; Subject; and a series of brief, numbered paragraphs. This format became a lifesaver in both my social work and on the job. Sure enough, after studying the report, that's the format I used.

While the nature of the data was confidential, there's no harm in pointing out certain failings that are common to all reporting systems. On my ex-job (see, that's how I've learned to think about it) there was the usual struggle with the department heads I had learned were 'data-lovers'. Their idea was that as long as we could transmit a great quantity of data, let's have a great quantity of data. But then, who reads it? And the first people to detect that no one is really reading and making use of the data are the people who are supposed to submit it. So they give timeliness and accuracy the low priority they feel it deserves. Then you have entry errors or entries that are so late they invalidate the timing of the report.

So where to start this particular assessment? I let my contact select the priority of my analysis by referring to the summary of our conversation. I reasoned that the criteria she was telling me were the areas she would like to see improved:

Thorough understanding of how data applies to operations management:

How much of the current data was necessary? My analysis showed that all products and services were individually tracked, despite the fact that 20% were responsible for 80% of branch volume.

Ability to design robust systems:

There was no way for me to tell just how much tweaking was going on, but with a report of this complexity, I could make an educated guess.

Experienced in strong team management:

This was my strength and what I felt was my strongest selling point as well. Bringing in an outsider was bound to cause a few ripples of resentment among the current staffers because the boss's comment was obvious: "I'm bringing in a heavy hitter because you guys can't cut it." I set out a detailed program of how I would deal with the motivational hurdles.

Know-how to design reports that answer questions rather than provoke them:

It was easy enough to guess who caught the flak when management had too many unanswered questions about the report: my contact. Once we had this project under way (notice how I'm already part of the team), it would be time to survey management and prioritize the data. Here, again, I set out a detailed description of my approach to research.

Experienced in meeting time and budget requirements:

Small wonder. My thinking was that if I got a project description, I would be halfway home. And I did. Any walk-through or paperwork would have me rounding third. I got that, too. So, after making my presentation, I was ready with my third question:

Me: How soon do you need this completed?

| **They:** | It all makes sense—up to the time chart. The only reason I would even consider taking this step is that I would I could show management an improvement sooner rather than later. |

Getting into the short strokes was like nothing—since I had come prepared to give. How much? I had prepared a 'negotiating question:

| **Me:** | How soon would you have to get this project done in order to get a medal? |

As I had hoped, my question got a laugh and a date—one I thought could be made. Now that I've given what was wanted, it was time for *me* to get:

Me:	What would be my compensation package?
They:	What do you mean by 'package?'
Me:	Well, there's my hourly fee, my expenses and a probable bonus if I beat the time and cost projections we've agreed on.

I figured there'd be no way that all three elements of my compensation would fly and I was right. For my fee, I simply took my past compensation calculated on an hourly basis and *doubled it*. After all, I wasn't a full-time employee and would be gone when the project was completed. If it seemed more practical to hire me full time at my previous salary that might be a consideration. Either way, I'd be working again.

Part 27:
Trouble shooting.

This is the part of the text where people look to see why whatever went wrong, went wrong.

When I didn't know anyone...

There were industries that were doing OK despite the economy—and some that were doing even better. The trouble was, that I didn't know anyone, or know anyone who knew anyone, or had never read anything by or about anyone in or near my specialty. So how do I find my contact? What I did was as logical as can be: I called the organizations I had targeted and asked for the names and titles of the decision-makers.

They:	Good morning, International Industries.
Me:	Good morning. I'm David Able, and I'm writing a letter to the head of your data department. Could you please tell me his or her name?
They:	That would be Claire Good-Kind
Me:	Is that C-L-A-I-R...?
They:	With an E at the end. And the last name is hyphenated. G-O-O-D hyphen K-I-N-D. She married, but kept her maiden name.
Me:	Thanks very much. What is Ms. Good-Kind's title, by the way?
They:	Director, MIS Department.
Me:	You've been very courteous and I'd like to tell that to Mrs. Good-kind. May I ask your name?...

Why all this detail about the simple procedure of getting or verifying a name? Wasn't everybody as friendly and cooperative as the previous example? Not really—and that was the problem. There was a time when organizations were very sensitive to the way in which their contact employees responded to the public. Many companies felt, and rightly so, that every caller was a potential customer, and should be treated accordingly. But good manners gave way to efficiency. Now I was lucky to get a live person instead of a toneless, 'there's-nobody-here-but-us-recordings' kind of voice that told me what button to press. And I was luckier still if the live person wasn't getting 10 calls a minute, had a personnel guide handy, and was someone for whom English was a first language.

The negative impact my research was trying to avoid was obvious. I wanted to send something that I hoped sounded personal enough to get through. An inaccurate name, gender or title would have meant a fast goodbye! So before I got ready to say, "hello," I got my script ready and practiced my best telephone voice. If, as I pointed out to my friends in the church basement, there was such a thing as 'rules for success' on the phone, they would read like this:

1. Introduce yourself. A busy receptionist is less likely to hang up on someone whose name they have just learned.

2. When they tell you the name of the potential contact, start spelling it immediately, so that you're sure you have it right. Don't say your thanks quite yet. To a busy receptionist, 'thank you' is the same as 'goodbye'.

3. Work from the script, so that in case you have to be put on hold you can come right back to the right spot.

4. Work from the script, so your conversation isn't slowed with "a-a-ahs." Respect the fact that the receptionist owes you nothing.

5. Work from the script, so that you'll remember how to compliment a helpful receptionist. Rudeness gets all the publicity. Let's say a few words on behalf of kindness and courtesy.

6. Work from the script so that in case you have to call an audible (a change of plan) you can do so. For example, the receptionist may be unable to get or give you the information you need. You'll have to be ready to ask to be transferred to the data department and start the script over again—with variations:

(I'm writing a letter to the head of your data department. Could you please tell me his or her name?)

7. Watch your word rate. Talking fast so that people won't hang up on you generally has the opposite effect. The more relaxed you sound, the more relaxed they'll be.

8. Watch your volume. Try not to sound any louder than the voice you're listening to. Otherwise, your conversation could take on the tone of an attack.

9. Watch your temper. Remember, it's a favor you're after, not an argument. Take deep breaths.

10. And never never never never interrupt. The reasons are too obvious to take any time for.

When my contact was an S.O.B....

Not everybody is a nice person. This didn't come as news to me and I hope it doesn't come as news to anyone else. There were times when I knew my paragraph was good, but my contact wasn't. Remember, you heard it here. Twice, for emphasis. Not everyone is a nice person. Not everyone is open to communications they haven't initiated. The higher they are on the ladder, the more people they have keeping everyone else down. And they all, to put it politely—play with the truth:

He or she never got the letter—as if the postal service failed yet again.

He or she is out of town, sick in bed, or stolen by gypsies.

He or she is at a meeting and will call you back when it's over.

I figured it this way: This person is so hard to reach, that anyone who *does* succeed in getting through would make a powerful impression. So I let my anger at Mr. Big take over. One of us was going to give up and it wasn't going to be me. What did I have to lose?

I first set out to find every bit of information I could about him: Google, the trade press, whatever. If there was a quote or a speech or an article signed off with his name, this was grist for my mill. I particularly favored speeches made before trade or professional groups. Then I, too, would play with the truth:

Mr. Belvedere Big
VP Information Management
Worldwide Trucking, Inc.
Wherever, USA

Dear Buddy,

That's what everyone was calling you at the September Worldwide meeting in Denver, so I took the liberty of doing the same. Chances are I was just a face in that crowd to you, but like many around me, I was listening closely and made note of a number of salient points.

I have, however, certain questions about how you went about 'reducing the cost of your data flow through better management.'

The rest of my letter followed in the usual way, after, I hoped, I had convinced the guardians that 'Buddy' was, indeed, my buddy. If my message got through to him and was still rejected, then my message needed improvement and I could change it for the next communication,

True, I had treated them the same way they had treated me: by playing with the truth. I wasn't at that convention in Denver. I did, however, locate a detailed report on Google, which not only recounted some key paragraphs of his talk, but described the audience reaction as well. It even provided his nickname. Mind you, the whole idea made me less than comfortable, but my anger at being ignored made up for a large part of that. Besides, for the cost of a stamp and a phone call, I could keep this up indefinitely.

The curse of the phone mail.

Whoever invented phone mail was probably some good-hearted person who was hoping this idea would improve communication and help to increase efficiency. Just imagine—no more lost messages. Isn't that wonderful? Whoever it was, I'd like to run him over with a truck. My reason? What may have started as a more efficient way to keep people in touch, has deteriorated into a way of keeping people at a distance. After I-don't-know-how-many unreturned calls, I realized the truth:

Phone mail is a screening device and I'm the one being screened.

When I've primed myself for a call, I've primed myself for a 'live' conversation, and not a talk into a recording machine.

If I expected to either be called back or allowed through the screen, I would need an offer the listener could not refuse.

If no amount of mannerly persistence got through, it was time for SOME-THING ELSE. The procedure I developed worked this way:

1. I began with the belief that the contact really wanted to meet with me and was simply unavailable at that time. I kept a script ready so that I could deliver my message in a friendly and positive voice, without a lot of 'ahhh-hhs.' The script reminded the contact of the key points of my Contact Communication and offered a choice of two meeting times.

2. If there is no call back to indicate that the contact had made a choice of meeting times, my first message ended with the promise to call again—so I did. This time my script said that I would be in the area (Thursday afternoon) and would be willing to come by on a 'standby basis' in case a few minutes opened up. If there is another day that would be better for such an arrangement, I asked for a call back. Otherwise, I would be there.

3. When a series of phone-mail contacts have proven to be non-productive, I make a sympathetic call. Anyone that busy or under that much pressure might welcome a time-saving lunch at his or her desk—a lunch that I would be happy to deliver and join. If there is some wonderful food source, I stress the advantages of enjoying that great take-out without losing any important time. I close this call with a choice of menu and ask for a call back, so that the contact could order the preferred meal.

4. If none of the above is successful, there are two ways to go. The first is to get angry enough to tell a whopper. Not a terrible lie, but a lie, nevertheless. So my next message was:

Me: Contacting you is the most difficult thing I've done since I went climbing in the Harz. It was supposed to be easy, with no climbs in the 10th grade—maybe not even the 9th. And the Brocken is only 1141 feet—with no hanging belays. Anyway, there I was, rappelling my way back, when I ran into an alcove that just wasn't indicated on any of my maps. What happened next? Well, I'm lucky to still be alive and making this call. So what do you say we keep my luck going? I can be at

your office this Thursday. Is early or late better for you?
I'll call tomorrow to find out—unless you call me first.

Why mountain climbing? Why not? Maybe I was inspired by the information that my contact was a climber, and I've done a bit of it myself. (Not to the extent indicated by my story, perhaps, but I said it was a whopper.) Or maybe it was simply to create a persona my contact would like to meet. In any event, if this one doesn't work, next time it's going to be a sailing story, or spelunking, or whatever I think will capture interest..

The second approach is to face the fact that the contact isn't buying what I'm selling. So, it's time to start over. I send a new Contact Communication with a new set of skills. If he/she doesn't want oranges, then how about apples? Or maybe grapefruit. Or pineapple. Everyone to their own taste.

Was I running the risk that these people might get pissed off at me? Of course! But *I* was already pissed off at *them*, so what difference did it make? However, here's the punch line: I got more than one appointment because, as one contact put it, "Anyone with your kind of persistence must be pretty confident about what he can do."

When I couldn't meet all the criteria...

There were some criteria I couldn't meet. This was bound to happen, since I was exploring fields in which I had no specific experience. While I did have a solid background in many aspects of data management, none of it, for example, was in the automotive aftermarket industry. As a rule, 'industry experience' was at the bottom of the list of criteria, but even if it wasn't, I left it for the last S-H-O-T.

Me: According to my notes, one of your criteria calls for automotive industry experience. Could you tell me why that's important?

The decision-maker would then explain how the particular criterion fits into the overall job. It may be a skill that I would be called upon to use directly. It may be a skill others use under my supervision. It may be a skill other members of the team will use and would depend on my familiarity to achieve the needed cooperation. For obvious reasons, I'd want a full understanding of a criterion before I explained how well I could meet it.

But suppose I *can't* meet it? Ignore it? Fudge the truth a bit? What then? What happens then is that I rely on the fact that I have already taken my S-H-O-T with all the other criteria and gotten positive responses to my test questions. I've just proven that I know a lot. Not everything, perhaps, but a lot.

Me: As to experience with the (XYZ Hi-Speed Communication System) the industry uses, I have no hands-on in my background. In your considered judgment, how long would it take someone with the skills I've presented, to master that system?

It sometimes turned out there was some hardware, software or underwear peculiar to the industry with which I had no hands-on experience. That happened. But it wasn't the end of the world. It wasn't even the end of the conversation. Rather than say I didn't know a thing about it, I referred to my 'lack of hands-on experience.' Chances are it was a variation of something I already knew about. But just to make sure, I asked:

Me: In your considered judgment, how long would it take someone with the skills I've presented to master that system?

Not just to learn it, mind, but to *master* it. When it comes to developing added skills, I don't fool around. Whatever the answer—be it hours, weeks or months, I'd be prepared to negotiate:

Me: Then if there was an opportunity for work, I would be willing to accept a lower rate of pay for that period. How well do you think that proposal would balance my lack of hands-on experience?

When I didn't understand some 'inside' term…

The first temptation is to fake it—to nod as if you understand, make a note of it and move on. I found this to be the most effective way to of getting the complete list of criteria. To interrupt with questions can also interrupt the flow of ideas. So I just nodded and made a note. (I didn't really fake it—that was a lie.) But when I was reviewing each criterion, I came back to it. For example, I had never heard of an OCM:

Me: You said that reports would be made to the OCM. Could you tell me more about that?

Could you tell me more about that?

That question doesn't admit, "I don't know what you're talking about." It simply says I need more information. I might then discover that OCM stood for Office of Corporation Management, or Operations Committee Meeting, or Opportunity for Critical Mention. I might even learn how these groups function in the organization's decision-making system and why it is so important to present the right kind of report. Asking for more information was more effective than pretending to understand, and gave me a chance to demonstrate that I was the kind of worker who would rather know than guess.

When it was time to prove I could do it...

Back in the days when I was hiring, (I never really appreciated the sound of that till now) I met a lot of what I used to call 'empty-handed geniuses.' They had copies of their resumes with them, of course—just in case I had had the one they sent me mounted and framed. And, of course, the resume was rich in recounting their responsibilities. Under closer questioning, however, these claims became less than convincing. Part of this was due to nervousness under the stress of the interview. Part of it was trying to recapture the details of a project that had happened a while back. But part of it was an exaggeration of the role the applicant played in the success of that project—or the level of success of the project itself.

So instead of joining the ranks of the empty-handed geniuses, I came to these conversations loaded for bear. I had, of course, my letters of recommendation, but I didn't stop there. I had before-and-after hard copies of reports, business plans, budget projections, work samples and anything that proved the skills I planned to present. I simply could not afford to leave any doubt that I was best qualified to help my contact reach his/her goals. By the time I was finished, I wanted them to stop seeing some middle-aged, balding guy and visualize instead their promotion to a corner office.

When I was tempted to 'top' the criterion...

At first, I wasn't aware just how many criteria had numbers in them: number of years of experience at a particular level of responsibility; number of people reporting to me; number of people in my department; number of accounts, branches, units of information, network stations managed. The temptation was always there to be better than what was required.

For example, what could be more reassuring during a conversation about marketing skills that listed a criterion of dealing with a customer base of 1,000, to reveal that *I* was accustomed to a customer base of *100,000*? The answer: plenty. I had, through my big mouth, made myself a big wheel—too big to carry the load they had in mind. In the same way, why not respond to 'the ability to manage a team of 6.' with the happy news that *I* have managed a team of *sixteen*. Isn't that better?

No, it isn't. By overpowering the criteria, I ran the risk of overpowering my contact. By matching the criteria, I matched the needs of my contact. I also learned not to pin a date on any of my achievements. Being a lot older than my contact was no advantage, either.

When I take the risk of asking for the work…

What I could never be sure of is just how well my contact appreciated the presentation of my skills. While I was careful to speak directly to the criteria he/she had provided, highlighted the appropriate experience and offered convincing proof to support what I was saying, it was often difficult for me to 'read' the reaction. Some contacts tried to avoid any kind of positive response because of the belief that any show of enthusiasm would weaken their bargaining position. With other contacts I didn't know how clearly he/she understood the information I had just communicated. Most important, there was no sure way of knowing how accurately my information met the particular criterion.

So I had to ask. My problem was that I couldn't ask for work directly—in so many words. What had set up this conversation was my desire to know the criteria for getting work, and a chance to verify how well my skills would match them. The test question after every criterion was as close as I dared to come. But when I encountered a sign of real interest, I felt I had no other choice but to go the distance:

May I see the project?

How soon do you need it?

What is the compensation package?

What I did not know was whether or not my contact would make the final decision. That's why, over the door of the Temple at Karnak, in the original Aramaic, is an inscription that reads: "Do not pray. Ask. You have a better chance of getting an answer."

Sometimes the answer made clear that my contact wanted me—or at least wanted the help I could provide—but would have a tough selling job 'upstairs.' When that happened it was time to remember that we were no longer on opposite sides of the desk, in a manner of speaking. We both wanted the same thing—me to come on board. The challenge was how to make this happy event come about. How do we work together? What help does the contact need from me? Once again, I'd better ask.

Me: Which of the information we've reviewed would help
                           to convince whoever might need convincing?

When it's time to talk money...

Management's job is to pay as little as possible for as much as possible. That
didn't come to me as big news because that was my own attitude at one time.
Now here I am at the receiving end. That's why I studied the want ads. Not that
I thought I'd find what I was looking for (if there was an interesting company I'd
research it, as I've already explained) but to see what was being asked for and how
much money was being offered. The winning ad, going away, required in-depth
familiarity with super-market food merchandising, specializing in freezer inven-
tory, display and promotion. In addition, the applicant would need extensive
experience in every phase of production and distribution of frozen fish, from the
fresh catch through every step of processing including packaging and pricing.
And, oh yes, complete fluency in speaking reading and writing Chinese. Finally,
if you think that rather amazing combination of talent would pay off big at compensation time, forget it. The money was not all that much.

   The moral is plain. Asking ain't getting. Like I said, it's management's job to
buy as many skills as possible for as little money as possible. Nothing wrong with
that. The term "as possible" suggests an opening for negotiation. Nothing wrong
with that, either.

   What I wanted was the opportunity to place my can-do's n some sort of balance my contact could then weigh in comparison to my cost. This was particularly important when some higher-up factored in the decision. Which is why I
learned to block-print BIG, so that the criteria took up a number of pages, and
that third party in the upstairs office could read them easily. Of course I would
have preferred to be introduced myself, and to determine the boss's criteria as
well, but I was supposed to be invisible, remember?

When the criteria are 'intangible'...

Don't let the phrase fool you. There ain't no such thing as 'equal opportunity.'
Some are always just a bit more equal than others. Each individual in the decision-making ladder from the lowliest apparatchik in personnel to the chairman of
the board, has an inner image of the kind of person they feel would 'fit in.' In
trade talk it's the 'halo affect'—the tendency to endow certain characteristics with
special qualities. These are generally expressed as a 'they' as in, "We don't want a
woman for this position because they...."

   "We're looking for a younger person because they...."

"We tend not to hire Jews (or Blacks or foreign born) because they...."

"We avoid overweight people because they...."

It's bias. In some cases, it's out and out bigotry. In all cases it's against the law. But in all too many cases, it *is* the law. And if we're over-age, female, Black, foreign-born, etc. we've been that way long enough to know enough to watch the face of the contact at the moment of first meeting and know what conclusion to draw.

Even if the decision-maker has the kind of poker face that could lead to wealth at a table in Vegas, there are verbal clues as well:

There was a guarded reluctance to answer my test questions.

The date the project was needed was evaded.

None of the problem-solving I presented generated any questions.

Which is why, when I sensed there may be an image problem, I found the best defense to be a good offense. What is up for grabs in this situation is who is in control—me or the bias. As I went through the social amenities, I silently recited my mantra: "Thanks to my research, the quality of my paragraph and follow up and that God was not busy in the Middle East that week, I am face to face with my contact. This means that while they may not have any work for me at the present time, I have enough skills to interest the contact in at least talking to me."

What happens next is up to me.

When my contact doesn't know the criteria...

Sure, it's a long shot, but there are contacts out there who just don't think in terms of specific criteria. When I asked the question, all I got in return was a blank stare. So, to provide thinking time, I asked for permission to take notes. Then I took my time block-printing the word CRITERIA on my pad. I took even more time drawing a line down the center of the page. Archimedes couldn't have done a neater job. Still nothing. I was now free to panic. But the contact spoke and I was saved.

Or so I thought. But what I got was the information that 'they wanted people who can cut it.' That's almost as specific as 'tell me about yourself.' So where do I go from there? It was then that I learned to initiate a dialogue:

| **Me:** | During my research about data gathering in the automobile aftermarket business, some people I talked to felt that it was important to know how to design a report that answers questions instead of provoking them. What's your feeling about that? |

Any question beginning with who, what, where, when, why and how couldn't be answered yes or no—or with a grunt. That meant a dialogue had to get under way. I had a criterion to make note of and to ask what was next. The contact could tell me (and did) that, in his considered judgment, there are a number of criteria far more important than the ability to design reports. Fair enough. What are they?

When a failure may not be a failure...

Learning from my mistakes made sense in the church basement, but when the mortgage payment was due, that whole idea really sucked. The sad fact is that I could not afford mistakes—not any more of them than I had already made. So I tried to distill a few drops of courage from my anger at being rejected—the courage to turn a 'no' into a 'yes.' I kept reminding myself that I had logic on my side. I had gotten to the point where I had learned the criteria and could meet them. I had the skills to provide 'more' for any work I was given: more profit; more efficiency; more economy; more of anything the typical organization might be looking for. Whatever costs I incurred would be an investment that would pay for itself. Since my discussions proved that I was what my contacts were on the lookout for, why didn't they find me enough of a reason to stop looking?

I began to see their refusal to make a commitment in terms of the context in which it was said. The contact who seemed convinced I was right for the work at hand but couldn't give me the go-ahead 'at this time' would still have a time problem in getting the work done. There I was, offering to do the assignment on a test basis. The way I figured it, both of us would be enjoying a number of advantages:

My contact would be getting the work done, getting a chance to test my abilities without making a long-term commitment, getting a chance to test my ability to work well with others on the team without getting involved in retirement plans, health benefits, etc.

Meanwhile, I would be getting a chance to see how I liked the work. I would be getting a chance to see how I liked the working environment while earning some money, while I can still keep looking for other work.

How much better could it get? All we needed was a starting gun, so I fired one:

Me: What else would you have to know in order to be convinced that I'm the right person and this is the right time?

That did it. I may not have gotten as much in the way of dollars as I wanted but I got back into action. I just wanted more, so, while I was working, I kept right on looking.

In a perfect world, I wouldn't have needed that killer question. I would have matched my skills to the contact's criteria, negotiated a starting date and compensation, shaken hands and gone out to a nice lunch. What I would have been describing at this point would have been the menu—or perhaps even the wine list. But this is not a perfect world. Each contact may be struggling with a decision that may have more layers than a Viennese torte. I could not help but begin to feel a conflict:

I wanted the work and they wanted the work done. There was usually no job open as such, so there was no competition for it. There was nothing else they wanted to know in order to be convinced. Some said they would let me know by Thursday. By Monday I still hadn't heard. Because it was just not a perfect world.

One thing is certain. I'm not sitting by the phone and waiting for it to ring. I'm not waiting for the angst to build to a point where I'd be tempted to give up the whole idea. I keep working and I keep looking for work. There is, of course, a downside to this procedure. I may wind up having to decide between too many work offers. But that's what happens when it's just not a perfect world.

0-595-31477-5